C0-CFJ-935

HOW TO GIVE A
BUTT
KICKING
PRESENTATION!

The Essential Handbook for Every Presenter

6/6/2011

Miss Anette!

Knock em Dead!

Best Wishes

Coach Pile.

Dr. Kimberly Alyn

© Copyright 2010 Dr. Kimberly Alyn
Printed in the United States of America
Higher House Publishing, San Luis Obispo, CA 93401

All rights reserved. No part of this publication may be reproduced or transmitted in any form or by any means electronic or mechanical, including photocopy, recording, or any information storage and retrieval system, without permission in writing from the copyright owner, Dr. Kimberly Alyn.

Requests for permission to make copies of any part of this work should be emailed to: Info@KimberlyAlyn.com.

ISBN: 978-0615309545

ABOUT THE
AUTHOR

Dr. Kimberly Alyn is a best-selling author and award-winning international professional speaker. Dr. Alyn provides powerful keynote presentations for conferences, associations, corporations, small businesses, and municipalities.

Dr. Alyn's sessions receive the highest ratings at conferences and events. She provides inspiration, humor, education, and passion to her dynamic presentations. Her years of experience have enabled her to pass along many valuable insights to other speakers and presenters. She is well-known for taking the driest of topics and turning them into fun and interesting presentations. She has also coached individuals and executive teams to higher levels of improvement in their public speaking skills.

In her popular presentations, Dr. Alyn tackles topics that every person and every organization can relate to, like rising to real leadership, inspiring others to achieve more, teambuilding, doing the right thing, taking risks, dealing with annoying people, facing your fears, having a sense of humor, and loving what you do in life!

Dr. Alyn is the author of ten books including the best-seller *How to Deal With Annoying People* (with Bob Phillips), *Discover your Inner Strength* (with contributors Stephen Covey, Ken Blanchard, and Brian Tracy), *How to Inspire People to Achieve More*, and *Men are Slobs, Women are Neat...and other Gender Lies that Damage Relationships* (with Bob Phillips). She has also developed and produced numerous CD/DVD productions on a variety of topics. Dr. Alyn has been a contributing author to a variety of magazines and has been quoted in prominent books and publications like *Cosmopolitan.*

Sunny central California is home to Dr. Alyn. This is where she enjoys spending time with her family and friends. She works hard, plays hard, and loves life!

If you would like more information on
Dr. Kimberly Alyn, go to her web site at:
KimberlyAlyn.com

You can reach Dr. Alyn through her
business manager via email at:
Info@KimberlyAlyn.com or 800-821-8116

You can connect with Dr. Alyn at:
Facebook.com/KimberlyAlyn
Twitter.com/KimberlyAlyn
LinkedIn.com/In/KimberlyAlyn

TABLE OF CONTENTS

INTRODUCTION

I never dreamed about being a professional speaker. In fact, there was a time in my life when that idea would have terrified me. I loathed getting in front of people. I hated giving presentations. I trembled at the thought of speaking to groups. My, my, how life has a way of changing things....

Giving butt kicking presentations takes a strong stomach and a resilient spirit. It takes commitment and perseverance. It takes time and patience. It is certainly not for wimps! This book is the result of years and years of overcoming my wimpy attitude about giving presentations and speaking in front of people. As you will soon discover, I was the biggest coward and the infamous wimp when it came to public speaking. If I can conquer that fear and all that comes with it and learn to give butt kicking presentations, anyone can!

The ability to communicate and articulate your thoughts and ideas to others is an invaluable skill. This skill alone will determine your level of success in any given endeavor. The Carnegie Institute of Technology reports that only 15% of your success in any given field is attributable to your technical knowledge. The remaining 85% is due to your ability to arouse enthusiasm, express ideas, and lead people.

Whether you are presenting an idea at work, running a meeting, pitching a product, speaking to large groups, or talking one-on-one, speaking and communication skills are a must. Your communication skills are much more important than your technical knowledge.

This book is designed to assist you in your quest to give better presentations. It is designed to help you overcome the fear of public speaking. Whether you are a beginning presenter or a seasoned one, you will gain some practical tools to improve your presentation skills.

Maybe you're only interested in facilitating better meetings. Perhaps your goal is to engage your listeners more when giving small or large presentations. Maybe you are striving to become a professional speaker. This book will provide many practical and useful tips and tools for accomplishing all of those goals and more.

You will have the opportunity to learn from the many mistakes I made along the way. It has been a long learning process discovering what engages an audience and what annoys them. I have learned from experience how to maintain a lively speaking environment, whether it's a twenty-minute speech or an eight-hour workshop.

I have solicited the feedback of thousands of audience members or other such victims who have been subjected to my presentations. Their input, ideas, and suggestions have been invaluable to me. There are no better experts on what constitutes a good presentation than those being subjected to the presentations. My style of speaking has evolved through the years as a direct result of a lot of feedback. You will have the luxury of gaining the insights on that feedback without having to conduct thousands of presentations to get it.

Giving presentations should be fun and rewarding, and it can be. With some practice, patience, and perseverance, you can become a polished speaker and presenter. It is my hope that this book will assist you in that process. I welcome your feedback on the concepts that you will encounter throughout the book. As you commit to improve your speaking and presentation skills, just remember the words of Brian Tracy:

"The future belongs to the risk-takers,
not the comfort-seekers."

1

AWAKENING THE TERROR WITHIN

"The oldest and strongest emotion of mankind is fear."
—H.P. Lovecraft

Glossophobia is the fear of public speaking. I think it's called this because your eyes "gloss" over as you become faint, dizzy, and short of breath. There seems to be a "phobia" for everything, but this one is *real*. Many people suffer from glossophobia and they may not even realize it until they are forced to stand in front of people and talk.

The first time I was ever asked to speak in front of a group, I was fourteen years old. I had no idea what "stage fright" was, nor had I been introduced to the fear of public speaking. I was about to meet sheer terror, and it would change the course of my life.

The request seemed simple enough. I was merely asked to narrate a school play. I would be standing at the side of the stage behind a lectern. A small microphone would extend from the lectern and a small light would illuminate my notes. I didn't even need to memorize any lines. How hard could this possibly be? I agreed to narrate the play as I grabbed the script and stuffed it in my backpack. I never even looked at it again. It just didn't seem that difficult to read the words printed on a piece of paper.

The night of the play arrived and I walked into the auditorium about fifteen minutes before the play started. I had my script rolled up in a tube which I proceeded to use as a "bonking" weapon to antagonize the actors behind the curtain. The director approached me and asked if I could take my place behind the lectern. I obliged and flattened out my script in front of me as I adjusted the microphone closer to my mouth.

I could hear the music beginning and I knew my cue to speak would be fast-approaching. I glanced out at the audience. There were at least two hundred people staring at the stage. An uncontrollable wave of anxiety began to sweep over my body. My legs began to tremble and my hands began to shake. My heart was pounding out of my chest and my pulse was racing at top speed. The saliva in my mouth began to evaporate and I started to feel faint.

The music stopped, which was my cue to begin speaking. At this point, I was thinking that I would rather be chewing tin foil than dealing with this anxiety. I glanced down at my notes and the words all seemed to blur together. I tried to focus my eyes as I swallowed hard and opened my mouth. What eeked out of me was the most horrifying sound as my voiced cracked and trembled with sheer terror.

I glanced again at the audience, hoping that by some miracle of God they had disappeared and this was all just some horrible nightmare. They were still there. I could see the pained look on every face in the audience as I fumbled over my words. I'm quite sure they were all waiting for my head to spin around. The play seemed to last forever, and every time I had to interject a narration, the audience cringed.

When the curtain finally closed, I took a deep breath, dropped my head in my hands and swore that I would *never* speak in front of a group again! I wondered how I would ever show my face in public after that disaster. I had failed and I had failed miserably. I walked away from the auditorium feeling completely debilitated and I was convinced that public speaking was not for me.

The Lasting Effects

The effects of that experience followed me for years. As I continued in high school, I refused to run for class office. As much as I enjoyed getting involved and taking a leadership role, I would not risk having to "give a speech." I avoided any assignments that required speaking in front of others. I reserved my opinion in groups or meetings in an effort to hide my anxiety. I did not want to relive that horrible experience and the anxiety that came with it. I avoided, dodged, and escaped any possible chance of having to speak in front of people. Until that one day many years later....

It was Sunday morning and I was sitting in church next to my husband. We were involved in the leadership of the church, but I steered clear of any "presentations." It was a very casual church with contemporary music and a laid-back atmosphere.

The service hadn't started yet and my husband got up from his seat to go to the restroom. While he was gone, the pastor walked by me and quickly asked me to give the announcements that morning. Giving the announcements would involve standing in front of a few hundred people and highlighting some items in the church bulletin.

Before I could respond to the pastor's request, he disappeared into another room. I sat in my chair in utter shock. My hands began to shake and I could feel the sweat starting to bead on my forehead. My heart was beating wildly in my chest.

My husband returned and sat next to me. I took a deep breath and reached over and took his hand. I said, "Honey, you are not going to believe what just happened. The pastor just came by here and he wants... well he needs... he was asking if..." I couldn't seem to get it out.

"He was asking *what,* Kim?" My husband was trying to be patient.

"Well, he wanted to know if *you* could give the announcements this morning." I couldn't look him in the eye as the words escaped from my lips.

"What?! I can't do that! I hate public speaking." Now *his* heart was beating wildly.

"Fine, I'll do it for you if you can't get up there and do it," I offered with a condescending tone.

"No, I don't need you to 'do it for me,'" he replied back snidely. "I will do it myself."

Relieved, I watched him fumble his way through the announcements much better than I would have, and I gave him an encouraging smile as he finished. When we got home that day, I confessed the truth to him. I don't know if he has ever forgiven me for that one!

That was the day I knew I had a problem. When it gets to the point where you are willing to lie in *church*, you know you need to face some issues. I had a phobia, and it was time to deal with it. I decided that the next time the pastor needed the announcements done, I would do it. It was a grueling experience for the audience, but I did it. I suffered through the fear and I pushed myself up to the front of that church. I knew if I ever really wanted to conquer this fear, I would have to challenge the fear on a consistent basis. The idea of that did not appeal to me.

There came a point not long after that experience that I had to make a critical decision. I would either have to master this fear, or I would have to set aside my business goals and settle for something less than what I really wanted. I did not want to be controlled by this fear. The decision I made would change the course of my life.

Taking the First Step

The first step is always the hardest. I owned a financial planning firm and I had just finished the long process of becoming certified. I felt like there was an enormous amount of information that was of such value to the public. I saw an inadequate amount of education available on the topics of financial planning and money management.

We weren't learning this stuff in high school and college. We were learning how to make money with our degrees and education, but we weren't learning what to do with that money once we earned it. I had a deep desire to educate the public about these issues. There was just one very big obstacle: I would have to get up in front of people and talk.

I had a critical decision to make. I would either have to give up this dream or I would have to conquer this fear. I wrestled with this dilemma for quite some time before I finally came to a resolution. I decided that I would not be mastered by my fear, but I would instead master the fear and achieve my dream.

I took the financial planning course that I wanted to teach to the local community college and asked them to consider it for the community education program. The course was twelve hours in length and would be spread over four sessions, one per week. The attendees would have to listen to me teach and instruct for three hours at a time! I had no idea how I could possibly pull this off, but I was willing to try.

The college accepted the proposal and added my class to their community education line-up. I was scheduled to teach one set of classes on Tuesday nights for four weeks and another set on Thursday nights. I had two months to prepare.

I invested in my own marketing brochure to ensure that the classes were well-attended. I compiled professional workbooks for the attendees. I invested thousands of dollars in an overhead projector (if you can imagine now!), a projection screen, a podium wrap, table cloths, and a long list of other items that would enhance the classroom environment.

The Time Draws Near

As the date of my first class drew closer, the fear began to paralyze me. I would wake up in a cold sweat after dreaming that no one showed up for class. I would wake up in a cold sweat after dreaming that the class was full of people. It was lose-lose for me. If no one showed up, I had a huge business loss to eat. If lots of people showed up, I had to speak and that was sure to cause my demise. *What if they hated me? What if they asked questions I couldn't answer? What if they sneered at me at the break and made snide remarks about my presentation? What if they thought the material was boring?* The "what-ifs" were making me crazy!

Four weeks prior to my first class I began practicing my presentations. I set up my overhead projector and screen in my living room. I lined up all the stuffed animals in the house I could find. I gave them the best I had. They were speechless. Regardless of their lack of feedback, I was determined to press on.

The night of the first class rolled around. Forty-two people had registered and I was terrified. I got some of my friends and clients to take the class to try and provide some level of comfort for me. It didn't help. I was still terrified. I was trembling, sweating, and shaking as I began the first session of my first class. It was very uncomfortable for me and the audience. But I pushed through it, and I completed the three-hour class and survived it!

The Feedback Begins

By the end of the first set of classes, I received some positive feedback from the attendees on the value of the information. I also received a lot of suggestions on the evaluation forms. Some of those included:

- Relax!
- Breathe
- Smile
- Lighten up
- Slow down – you talk a hundred miles per hour!
- You pace back and forth too much
- Repeat the questions from the audience
- Stand up straight

- Keep your hair out of your eyes
- Don't lean on the table
- Don't sit on the table
- Be careful who you poke fun at
- Stop using jargon we don't understand
- Give more breaks
- Have more interaction
- Leave more time for questions at the end
- Stop messing with your eye glasses
- Stop fidgeting with your pen
- Stop saying "um"
- Make more eye contact with the audience
- Let the audience share more of their experiences
- You scratch your neck a lot
- Don't ever pop your knuckles again!
- You stand in front of the projection screen and block it
- Put less information on the slides
- Try not to be so dependent on your slides
- Don't read the slides to us
- Add more humor to your presentation
- End the session a lit bit earlier
- Turn down the air conditioning
- Could we have more chocolate chip cookies?

It's amazing the feedback you will get when you ask for it and let people know you really do want to improve. They are much more likely to give you honest, useful, and constructive feedback. It didn't take long for me to start implementing some of those suggestions. It did take me quite some time to desensitize from the fear of being in front of people and talking or even "performing." It's intimidating to have all eyes on you knowing that everyone expects you to say something worth hearing.

Pushing Forward

Over the next year, I ruined many nice silk suits due to profuse sweating. That seemed to be my major outlet for nervousness. I realized through that period of time that there was only one way to get over the fear of public speaking: *do it*! Dale Carnegie has a great quote that I learned to adopt in my quest to conquer this fear:

"If you want to develop courage, do the thing you fear and keep on doing it until you have a record of successful experiences behind you. That is the quickest and surest way yet discovered to conquer fear."

That's exactly what I did. I kept doing what I feared until I no longer feared it. I built my financial planning practice through those educational seminars. Each and every session got better and better as I became more comfortable and implemented the suggestions of my attendees.

I stayed on top of the technical advancements and upgraded my equipment along the way as well. I graduated from the overhead projector to a laptop computer and LCD panel. The LCD panel connected to my laptop computer and sat on top of the overhead projector. LCD *projectors* were not common back then. That cheesy LCD panel cost me $6,000 (a boat load of money back then!) and became obsolete within one year. I converted my presentation from overheads to PowerPoint. I upgraded to an LCD projector and eventually integrated a cutting edge technological advancement: a remote control interactive learning system that was unheard of in seminar training at the time.

Had I not taken that first step to begin teaching those classes, I would not be doing what I do today. I would not be a professional speaker, and I would not be a professional training instructor. That first step changed the course of my life, and I will always be thankful that I pushed through the fear and endured the pain that it took to overcome my obstacles. It took me a good three years to realize that I loved giving presentations.

In the many years that I taught those classes, I began to receive invitations to speak in organizations on a variety of topics. One of those topics was public speaking and giving presentations. I began to teach at firefighter conferences and organizational events. I started to receive requests for other training classes and speech topics. I had become comfortable with teaching my financial planning classes through the college and it was time to push my limits.

I ventured out into the realm of professional speaking and it completely changed my life. I realized what a joy it had become to entertain, inspire, motivate, teach, and interact with different audiences. The pressure to perform certainly increases when you start charging people to hear you speak!

Each and every time I spoke, the anxiety and fear would dissipate even more. As I began to see the response from a variety of audiences, I realized what kept people interested and what bored them. My limits were stretched each and every time I got in front of a group of people.

I never imagined that I could be a professional speaker. That was not a possibility I thought I possessed. That's like telling someone with claustrophobia that they will someday be an elevator operator for one of the busiest hotels in New York City! I was truly phobic about public speaking, and I never could have fathomed becoming a professional speaker.

I finally came to the realization that I had possibilities within me that I had not fully explored. I realized I could overcome any fear with enough commitment and perseverance. We all have within us an amazing ability to accomplish great things.

"We all have possibilities we don't know about.
We can do things we don't even dream we could do."
—Dale Carnegie

2

WHAT IS EVERYONE SO AFRAID OF?

"No passion so effectually robs the mind of all of its powers of acting and reasoning as fear."
—*Edmund Burke*

While sport fishing off the Florida coast, a tourist capsized his boat. He could swim, but his extreme fear of alligators kept him clinging to the overturned craft. Spotting an old beachcomber standing on the shore, the tourist shouted, "Are there any gators around here?!"

"Naw," the man hollered back, "They ain't been around for years!"

Feeling safe, the tourist started swimming leisurely toward the shore. About halfway there he asked the guy, "How'd you get rid of the gators?"

"We didn't do nothin'," the beachcomber said.

"Wow," said the tourist.

The beachcomber added, "The sharks got 'em."

Fear is a debilitating emotion. You cannot rationalize or negotiate with fear. Many surveys have been conducted on what people fear, and public speaking almost always ranks number one! So what is it about public speaking that has people so afraid? Why are phobias developed over this issue? Why do people go to great lengths to avoid getting in front of people and speaking or presenting?

There are many reasons that people fear public speaking. While different people have different, specific reasons for being afraid of speaking, there are seven main reasons we are so afraid of public speaking:

1) Fear of the Unknown

For most people, it is an anomaly to get in front of people and speak. It is not something they do on a regular basis, so the fear of the unknown takes over. People do not have a track record of how others respond to them in this type of setting on a regular basis, so apprehension sets in. Most of the other activities that people engage in on a daily basis are routine. Because these activities are routine, there is no fear of the unknown adding additional stress to the situation. If an individual were conditioned at a very young age to speak in front of people regularly, there would be no apprehension or stress. It would just be considered part of the normal "routine" in life.

Think for a moment about some of the anxiety you have had over certain issues in your life. Maybe it was an interview for a job or the first day of a new job. Stress, fear, and anxiety set in because you are unsure of the outcome. We all want a level of certainty in our lives and we would all like the luxury of knowing the outcome, especially when we put our pride on the line. If we are certain, or even remotely certain of the outcome, we tend to feel more confident and less fearful.

I was once terrified of small planes. The thought of crawling into a very small and confined space and then climbing thousands of feet in the air did not appeal to me. This fear went hand-in-hand with my fear of heights. I suppose that fear went hand-in-hand with my fear of rollercoaster rides as well. I knew there was only one sure way to overcome my fears: do the very thing that I feared over and over until it was no longer "unknown to me."

I conquered my fear of rollercoasters by allowing my teenage son, Josh, to subject me to some of the scariest rides in the world! I did this over and over until I knew what to expect. After enough familiarity with the rides, I no longer felt as if I would throw up from fear and anxiety.

I conquered my fear of heights and small planes at the same time. I decided to get my pilot's license. That was probably one of the most difficult things I ever attempted in light of my extreme fear. As more and more time passed, I became more and more comfortable with each and every lesson. Getting behind that yoke for the first time and taking off was completely terrifying though! My instructor thought I needed professional help and medication, and he wondered why I was trying to get my license. I stuck with it, in spite of my fear, and finally walked away with my pilot's license.

The familiarity of public speaking is what dissipates fear. Once we know the outcome, there is no more fear of the unknown. Once we actually go through the process of making fools of ourselves, or bombing during a presentation, we have endured the worst. We realize that we can survive it and move on. We can get up and present again. We can improve and become better presenters. The process of doing it over and over creates a greater sense of comfort and ease.

2) Center of Attention

While it may seem that certain people like to be the center of attention, it is usually entirely different when speaking in public. As the speaker, you are all alone in the front of a room, or on a stage, and all eyes are focused on you. It's quiet and intimidating. Everyone is hanging on your every word or waiting for you to speak. You feel isolated and vulnerable.

If you had ten friends standing up there with you, the pressure would be relieved because you wouldn't feel like you were the center of attention. People tend to take more risks when the focus is not centered on them alone. You will have a much higher chance of dragging a group of people onto a stage versus dragging one person to stand up and perform. If we bomb, it's easier to have someone else bomb with us. The pressure of being the only one talking with everyone else listening causes a sense of fear to come over our bodies.

Good speakers learn to overcome this fear and capitalize on being the center of attention. As a speaker in front of a group, you have a rare opportunity to educate, inspire, motivate, or entertain your audience. Besides, this is your chance to talk and not have anyone interrupt you!

3) Pressure to Perform

As the person who is standing at the front speaking, you experience the immense pressure to perform. You feel a burden to please the audience and have something worthwhile to say. You may even feel the pressure to be funny or witty. People often have a difficult time just relaxing and trying to be themselves as they speak because of this pressure to perform.

When a tentative speaker looks out at the audience and sees a few apathetic or unfriendly faces, the pressure to perform increases. Speakers often feel like everyone needs to be smiling, laughing, or at least have an agreeable disposition.

When a speaker becomes more experienced and knowledgeable of how different audiences respond, this pressure to perform subsides. When the pressure to perform is lifted, the speakers can relax, be themselves, and have a good time. When this occurs, fear diminishes and performance actually skyrockets.

4) Lack of Confidence

Fear is fed when confidence is starved. If we are dwelling on our perceived inadequacies, fear will take over. If we compare ourselves to better speakers and magnify our shortcomings in our own minds, our performance will suffer. We become fearful of speaking in front of others if we are not confident in our knowledge on the topic or ability to deliver the presentation.

I have seen many speakers "psych" themselves out in a speaker line-up. Maybe the first speaker was very humorous and had the audience laughing constantly. The second speaker listens and becomes fearful that the audience will expect the same from him. To make matters worse, the speaker then sets himself up for failure. He walks in front of the group and says something like, "Well, I just have to apologize in advance, because that is a tough act to follow. I am not nearly as funny as that last speaker, so I guess you're stuck with me now."

You can actually see the audience lower their expectations at that point and start to slump in their chairs. The speaker just popped any bubbles of anticipation and enthusiasm that may have existed. Comparing ourselves to other speakers can hurt our confidence. When we attempt to take on the style of another speaker, we sacrifice our own unique style. This hurts the delivery of our presentations.

On the other hand, projecting confidence inspires confidence in your audience. When you exude enthusiasm and self-assurance, the audience will pick up on that and feel more comfortable with you. Even when you aren't feeling confident, at least *act* confident and the feelings will follow. Maybe you've heard the saying, "Fake it until you make it." I think that would apply here.

5) Failure Factor

We become fearful of speaking in front of people because we may fail. We might choke and forget what to say. We might bomb in our attempts at humor. The audience may fall asleep or display apathy towards our topic. People might get up and leave in the middle of the presentation. Nobody wants to fail, and if we perceive that as a high probability, we will fear public speaking and avoid it, if at all possible.

Experience in public speaking will reveal to any speaker that minor failures are inevitable. There will always be situations where the foot goes in the mouth, or the equipment fails, or we forget what we were going to say. As long as we learn to laugh at ourselves and enjoy the experience, the audience will not hold it against us.

It is through our failures that we become better presenters. All great success stories in life have been preceded by some form of failure. We need to learn to view failure as a tool for success, not a detriment or roadblock. When you play a game of chess, there are points in the game where you have to be willing to experience temporary failure to move towards ultimate victory. Sometimes you have to move backward to free up a move forward.

Most people who give up on public speaking or giving presentations do so out of a lack of perseverance. It's not usually a lack of skill or technique, because both of those areas can be improved. Instead, the fear of failure overcomes the will of a person and the motivation to persevere is assassinated. It is not until we can accept the failures in our lives that we can experience the victories.

"To begin to think with purpose is to enter the ranks of those strong ones who only recognize failure as one of the pathways to attainment."
—*James Allen*

6) Self-Absorption

I had just finished giving a presentation at a corporation. A middle-aged man approached me shyly and said, "I have always wanted to give presentations, but I can't stand looking at myself, so I know that no one else would either. I'm too short, too chubby, and too bald. I would just annoy everyone."

As I started talking to him, he lightened up and began to joke about some of his "flaws." He had me in stitches. He had a passion to speak about sales techniques, and he was very educated on his subject matter. I tried to explain to him that he could be an outstanding presenter if he would just lose some of his self-consciousness and self-absorption. He had never looked at himself as self-absorbed. Most people only consider conceited and vain people to be self-absorbed. Anyone who spends a great deal of time focusing on themselves instead of their topic or their audience is self-absorbed.

This man had a great opportunity to use humor in his presentations, and he could use the best humor there is: self-deprecation. When you can laugh at yourself and make people laugh, you have won over your audience. It shows your humanity and realness. Audiences cannot relate to people who are without flaws or who present themselves as such. We all know that no one is perfect, but we love to hear the speaker tell us or show us that in a humorous way.

One of the main reasons we are so fearful of public speaking is because we are so self-absorbed with how we will look. We are self-conscious about everything. We don't want to sound stupid or look stupid. Our complete focus on ourselves instead of our topic causes anxiety and fear. How many times have you told someone, "I don't care what other people think"? The fact is, we all care when we are up in front of a room full of people.

What if someone notices how big my nose is? What if the bald spot on the top of my head shows? What if I look like I am slouching? What if my mannerisms seem forced and awkward? The obsession with self-focused thoughts will cause any speaker to appear awkward and uncomfortable.

Once you transition your focus to your message instead of yourself, your fear will begin to dissipate as you put all of your energy into delivering your presentation with passion. Once you do this, your mannerisms, gestures, and delivery will flow naturally. The key is learning to get your mind off of you and your self-consciousness and on to your message. Then you can lighten up and actually enjoy the process. If you can learn to poke a little fun at your imperfections, the audience will find you more real and much more likable.

7) Misconceptions

When I walked to the front of the classroom, I was terrified. It was my first presentation at the local college, and there were over forty people in the classroom. I was about to give a three-hour presentation on some basic financial planning concepts. This same group of people would be returning the following week for another three hours. I had a lot of talking to do, and some very serious fears were rolling around in my brain.

What if I can't answer some of their questions? I'm sure there are people sitting here that know more about this than I do. I bet that guy in the front row is just waiting for me to say something stupid so he can pounce on my inadequacies. None of these people really want to hear what I have to say. I'm sure they are all here because their spouse made them attend!

It took me awhile to realize how wrong I was about everything. These people wanted to hear what I had to say, they wanted me to succeed, and they were all glad they attended. When I finally changed some of my misconceptions, much of the fear dissipated as I began to teach and present with confidence.

A tremendous amount of public speaking fear is attributable to misconceptions. People often feel like the audience will be overly critical of their presentation. In most cases, the speakers are much more critical of themselves than the audience. Speakers often fear that audience members may know more about the subject than the speaker. In most cases, even the people who do know more than the speaker will still learn *something*.

Another misconception that people have is that the members of the audience are just waiting for the speaker to fail miserably. The truth is, the audience wants you to succeed. The audience feels pain when you feel pain. They want you to enjoy speaking and they want you to have fun at it. They are sitting in their seats rooting for you, and you just need to change your perception to see that. Give yourself and the audience a chance!

Fear Can Become Phobic

*"I suffer from two phobias: 1) Phobia-phobia,
the fear that you're unable to get scared, and
2) Xylophataquieopiaphobia, the fear of not
pronouncing words correctly."*
—*Brad Stine*

Extreme fears lead to phobias, which can lead to obsessive behavior in an effort to avoid that which we fear. I am speaking from experience here. I had a major phobia when it came to public speaking, and I would go to great lengths to avoid any situation that would cause me to face my fear.

The fear turned into a phobia because I continued to feed the fear. I would allow my mind to dwell on the negative experiences I had in the past. I would think about other people that got up to speak and completely failed. I watched them flounder, sweat, and die a slow death in front of hundreds of people. I didn't want to subject myself to *that*!

The more I thought about the negative experiences I had and the negative experiences I witnessed in others, the more fearful I felt about speaking. It wasn't until I took control of my thought process that I was able to squash the fear. It took me a long time to view public speaking in a positive light, but I finally did. I began to think about great speakers and what it took them to become great speakers. Nearly all good speakers were at some point fearful of public speaking. Most great speakers had to really develop the skill and will to get up in front of people and present with style. Some of those great speakers even had to conquer phobias about public speaking.

Nearly all phobias are treated in one of two ways, or both: 1) medication and 2) desensitizing activities. Medication is used to suppress the physical panic aspects of phobic response, and the desensitizing activities are used to remove the fear of the unknown. While I wouldn't suggest medication for public speaking, I would highly recommend the second method: desensitizing activities.

The best way to overcome the fear or phobia of getting up in front of people is to *do it*! The next section will provide you with some practical tools to overcome the fear of public speaking.

3

OVERCOMING THE FEAR

"Courage is resistance to fear, and mastery of fear—not absence of fear. Except a creature be part coward, it is not a compliment to say it is brave."
—*Mark Twain*

The fear of public speaking is a direct result of conditioned response. We have conditioned ourselves to respond with anxiety when thinking about public speaking. As a result, we associate public speaking with fear and anxiety. Therefore, when we get up in front of people to speak, we have conditioned ourselves to respond with stress, fear, and apprehension.

I was teaching a seminar to a large group of firefighters one day. I asked the audience a question. "Does anyone know why a full-grown circus elephant can be clamped at the ankle and chained to a very small pole and the elephant will never try to pull away or escape?"

One brave firefighter offered his best guess: "Because he's married?" After the laughter subsided, I explained this phenomenon. When circus elephants are young and tiny, they are clamped at the ankle and chained to a pole. They try to pull away, but they are not strong enough, so they fail. They continue to try and continue to fail until they just stop trying. They are mentally conditioned to believe that they are not strong enough to escape. The elephant grows into an enormous animal that could yank that pole out of the ground with one good tug, but the elephant never even tries. He has conditioned himself to a state of learned helplessness.

Radio electrical fences create this same type of conditioning in dogs. An invisible fence is set up around the perimeter of the property with radio signals being sent to each receiver. The dog is equipped with a collar that sends a good shock to the dog if he attempts to cross the boundaries. As a result, the dog establishes a conditioned response and avoids the shock. You can remove the collar and the property markers and the dog will continue to stay within the boundaries.

Humans create a state of learned helplessness as well. Many people have established an invisible electrical fence in their lives when it comes to public speaking. They have associated stress and fear so closely with public speaking that they invariably assume they will receive that shock if they approach those boundaries. Years of mental conditioning have created chains of habit and most assume they are not strong enough to break those chains.

There is good news. Learned responses can be unlearned. New conditioning can drive out old conditioning. New habits can drive out old habits. The negative association can be re-programmed to a positive association.

There are some basic techniques that you can employ to cope with pre-speech anxiety and jitters. Those will be addressed in a later section. This portion deals primarily with overcoming the general fear of public speaking or giving presentations. There are three main ways to overcome the fear of public speaking and re-condition your thinking:

1) Change Your Association

The fear of public speaking is a direct result of a negative association. When most people think about having to give a presentation, they begin to think about all the things that could go wrong. They mull over the prospects of making a fool of themselves. They dwell on the idea that they will fail. They contemplate the concept that no one will like their presentation.

As these thoughts continue to swim around in the brain, the body provides a physical response as a result of the mental messages that are sent by the brain. There is a direct link established between public speaking and fear. An association is established between stress and giving presentations.

The mind is a very powerful tool. It works in conjunction with the body to create conditioned responses. When you create a negative association in your mind, your body responds with a negative reaction. When the time approaches to give your speech, your body is already conditioned to respond with anxiety, stress, worry, and fear.

You can actually re-train your mind and body to associate public speaking with calmness, fun, and enjoyment. I know that seems like a stretch when you are gripped with fear, but I am speaking from experience. I spent years and years of my life associating speaking with stress and anxiety, and it was a very difficult task for me to give a presentation. Today, I associate speaking with complete exhilaration and joy! I truly love it, and I never thought that would be possible.

So how do you change your association? You must re-train your mind. I spent a tremendous amount of time re-training my mind. I would go to the beach and sit quietly in a chair. I would close my eyes and picture my presentation. I could see the audience smiling and laughing. I saw myself at ease and enjoying myself. I could see people approaching me afterwards and thanking me for the valuable information. I began to picture the positive responses of my body: a relaxed posture, a calm, but enthusiastic tone, a confident stance, and natural gestures.

I could feel my heart rate slow down. I could feel my body relax. I began to re-condition my body to respond in a positive manner as a result of my positive association. When it came time for me to give a presentation, my mind and body accessed my new positive association, and my body responded accordingly. This process took a lot of time and energy, but believe me, it worked!

Learning to associate pleasure with speaking is the first step to overcoming the fear. If all of your associations are painful, you will avoid the experience. Even if your past experiences have been negative ones, you can still change your association. We all have more control over our responses and associations than we give ourselves credit for.

"Any idea, plan, or purpose may be placed in the mind through repetition of thought."
—*Napolean Hill*

2) Practice

This is where the desensitizing activities come in. Desensitizing activities will also assist you in changing your negative association to a positive one. I was once terrified of a huge rollercoaster ride at Knotts Berry Farm in California. It had upside down loops and was enormous. Whenever I approached the ride, my heart rate would quicken, I would feel sick to my stomach, and I would begin to sweat. It terrified me. I associated that ride with fear and terror.

One day I decided to slay this dragon. I was well into my twenties and I thought it was time to act like a brave adult. I was going to conquer that rollercoaster once and for all. I stood in line with my sister, trembling like a frightened child. I held her hand and whined all the way to the front of the line. I was sick to my stomach by the time we were strapped in. I closed my eyes and held on for dear life. I was too terrified to even scream. I never opened my eyes. Within a few minutes (which seemed like hours), we came to a screeching halt. I quickly scurried out of my seat and ran for the exit. My sister was right behind me.

She forced me back into the line and convinced me that one ride would not cure me. She insisted I would have to do it again and again until I could keep my eyes open and hold my hands up in the air. Right! Like *that* was ever going to happen!

We got back in line and rode again. I still didn't open my eyes and I was just as anxious to get off the ride. Then we rode again. My eyes were sealed shut, but I found the freedom to open my mouth and scream. It felt good. My stomach ache started to subside.

We rode it again. My heart rate was down below 200 now, so maybe I could open my eyes. I kept them open until we hit the first loop. Gripped by fear, I immediately closed them as tight as I could and held my breath. I didn't open them again until the ride ended.

We continued to get back in line and ride that one ride over and over. By about the sixth ride, I was able to keep my eyes open the entire time. By about the tenth ride, I knew exactly what to expect and I was waving my hands over my head screaming with delight! In one short day, I had completely changed my association from fear and terror to complete exhilaration and fun.

Whenever I walk by that ride now, my heart still races, but it's not with fear and terror—it races with the association of exhilaration and excitement. I can feel the thrill of the ride whenever I think about it.

That is by far the most effective and practical way to desensitize from any fear. Do that which you fear. As you become familiar with what to expect, the fear dissipates and your association changes. There was nothing more effective in getting me over my fear of public speaking than doing it over and over and over. I had to ride that rollercoaster of fear when it came to public speaking. The more I rode, the more comfortable I became. I knew what to expect and my anxiety subsided. My heart would still quicken before speaking, but the association was positive, not negative. I even got to the point where I would speak with my eyes *open* and my hands over my head!

If you truly want to overcome the fear of speaking, then speak. Speak a lot. If you truly want to overcome the fear of giving presentations, then give presentations. Give a lot of them. There is no better or faster way to overcome fear.

> *"Practice is the best of all instructors."*
> —*Publilius Syrus*

3) Preparation

There are many things you can do to prepare to give a speech. Those techniques will be addressed in later sections. When I talk about preparation here, I am talking about preparing to be a good presenter or speaker. If you plan to give lots of presentations or speak in front of people frequently, then this information will be valuable to you. If you only plan to stand up in front of people once a year, then you may not find this as useful. However, I will say this: if you want to give a good speech or presentation, you should probably practice before that "once-a-year" gig rolls around!

Preparing to be a better speaker takes more than knowing your material and memorizing your lines. It takes a little bit of time and commitment. One of the best things you can do to prepare to be a better speaker or presenter is to get a mentor. Find someone who speaks a lot and is good at it. Ask that person to spend some time with you. Find out what hurdles he/she had to overcome. Ask that person to watch you present and give you some pointers.

Some people don't seem to have the time for this. Instead, they continue to give presentations that irritate their audience, and the main point of the presentation is lost. Or some people have too much pride to ask someone else for help. They have a hard time admitting they need help. All speakers have room for improvement, and asking someone else to critique you will place you on a fast-track to better speaking.

Another way to prepare to be a better speaker and presenter is to go and watch other presentations. Evaluate other speakers and find out what the audience likes. This doesn't mean that you are trying to take on another speaker's style. Instead, it means you are adapting some of their *techniques* to your own style in order to improve. For example, you might observe another speaker who has mastered the use of PowerPoint in the presentation. The speaker has struck a great balance between using PowerPoint and still engaging the audience. You might be able to pick up some ideas on how to do that.

Another example: you might attend a conference and hear great feedback about a particular presentation. You might sit in on the class, and you see that the speaker has a real knack for interactivity with the audience and the use of humor. You might take notes on what makes the audience laugh and what keeps their attention.

People enjoy certain speakers and presentations for a reason. It doesn't happen by chance. As you study not only the speakers, but also the audience response, you can gather a wealth of information on which techniques fit your style and can be incorporated. You will also discover what doesn't fit your style or what doesn't come naturally to you. You may discover that incorporating small magic tricks into your presentation will liven it up. You might also discover that you have two left hands and juggling will never work for you. You may see a speaker use dry humor that works really well, but it doesn't fit your style.

The key to preparation is understanding what people want in a presentation and a speaker. You must understand who you will be presenting to and the uniqueness of each audience. For example, all-male audiences respond differently than all-female audiences.

Preparation requires that you put a little time and energy into becoming a better presenter. It is time well-spent.

"When you're prepared, you're more confident.
When you have a strategy, you're more comfortable."
—*Fred Couples, Professional Golfer*

Overcoming the fear of public speaking is not an overnight process. It requires a systematic and committed approach. It requires a lot of sweat and perseverance. If you can conquer the three techniques above, you are well on your way to giving great presentations.

Once you have conditioned your mind for public speaking, you can start dealing with the basics of a good presentation and your actual delivery. Before we look at those issues, let's dispel the common myths about public speaking in the next section.

4

COMMON MYTHS ABOUT PUBLIC SPEAKING

*"Preconceived notions are the locks
on the door to wisdom."*
—*Merry Browne*

There are a number of myths about public speaking. These myths often keep people from stepping out and taking a chance. When we hold tightly to preconceived ideas that are not always grounded in reality, we limit our capabilities. The preconceived ideas and myths don't just include the thought that we can't do it... sometimes the myths are just the opposite—we think it's too easy and we don't need to prepare.

There are many misconceptions and myths associated with public speaking. If you can dispel some of these myths in your own mind, you can clear the path to better presentations. Following are the six most common myths about public speaking.

Myth #1: Good Speakers are Born, Not Made

The reality is far from the myth. Some of the best speakers in the world spent years fine-tuning their speaking skills. If you talk to any seasoned speaker, chances are pretty high that this person experienced the same anxiety as everyone else in the initial stages of giving presentations. Nearly all public speakers have had to go through a process of becoming comfortable and at ease in front of people.

Some of the best speakers in history weren't born that way. Winston Churchill is known as one of the most eloquent speakers known to man. His command of the English language was legendary. He coined expressions that are now household phrases. When he stood before an audience, people leaned forward and soaked in every word. Was he born with a gift? No he wasn't.

Churchill agonized over his speeches when he first began. He actually threw up after one of his first speeches in the House of Commons. He spent hours putting his speeches together and invested a tremendous amount of time practicing each speech. He chose each and every word with careful consideration.

Churchill often gave controversial speeches that weren't always well received by every member in the audience. However, he came to be regarded as such a great speaker because he spoke with passion and conviction. He learned how to identify with the feelings of the audience and make a connection on some level. He was uncompromising in his presentation, and he worked at it until he mastered the art of public speaking.

Abraham Lincoln became known as an incredible orator. This was not a skill he was born with either. His beginning speeches and debates were often awkward and uncomfortable. He would keep his hands in his pockets or clasp them behind his back. It wasn't until he gained valuable experience through public speaking that he was able to relax and free up his gestures. Some of his initial speeches began with a squeaking, unpleasant voice. He had to learn to relax like everyone has to learn to relax.

Lincoln labored over his speeches much like Churchill. Lincoln was known to come up with ideas on the spur of the moment and jot them down. He would store them in his hat until he could formulate a speech later. He memorized most of his speeches and spent a good deal of time in preparation. Lincoln became a good speaker through practice, preparation, and experience.

Mastering any skill in life takes a commitment of time and energy. You must have a vision and a purpose for the skill. It doesn't matter if the thought of getting in front of people makes you throw up—you can still overcome the fear and master the skill. Winston Churchill and Abraham Lincoln proved that!

Myth #2: Good Speakers Don't Get Nervous

Feeling a sense of nervousness when having to speak in front of people is normal, even for prominent speakers. It surprises people to know that many famous presenters throughout history have struggled with feeling nervous when they speak publicly. Some examples include: Abraham Lincoln, Oprah Winfrey, Winston Churchill, Conan O'Brien, and Jay Leno. Many performers are fearful of having to give speeches. Leonardo Dicaprio experienced anxiety over public speaking early in his career. He secretly wished he wouldn't win an award just so he would not have to give an acceptance speech.

Mark Twain once said, "There are two types of speakers: those that are nervous and those that are liars." Some of the best speakers in the world still experience butterflies and sweaty palms before getting in front of a group. In almost all cases, you never look as nervous as you feel. If harnessed and handled properly, most people will never even know you are experiencing nervousness. Maybe those who know you very well will see a difference, but audience members who have never met you will not usually pick up on minor signs of nervousness.

While I have learned to harness my nervousness while speaking, I still feel a little bit of that anxiety just before I speak. It provides the extra adrenaline I need to give a powerful presentation. Nervousness is not your enemy. You just need to learn how to use it to your benefit. I will discuss some good techniques for dealing with nervousness in a later section.

Myth #3: My Presentations Have to be Formal

Many people are under the impression that public speeches and presentations have to be formal in nature. While there is a place for formal speeches, most presentations can have an element of informality to them. One speech or presentation can vacillate between serious and funny, all in the same speech. Moving an audience back and forth on the pendulum of emotion can make for an impacting presentation.

It's perfectly acceptable to take your subject matter seriously without taking yourself too seriously. Many speakers get up in front of people and assume they must be ultra serious to be taken seriously. This is not the case. You can be an expert on your subject matter and still present it in a fun and engaging manner. Poking fun at yourself shows the audience that you are human and vulnerable. Humor is a valuable tool in speaking and conveys a sense of realness to the audience.

Speakers can deliver professional speeches and presentations without being overly serious and ultra formal. A long, drawn-out formal speech that is void of any humor or variety will put an audience to sleep! I have made this very mistake when I first starting speaking. I began to realize that my audience was starved for a little informality, humor, and relaxation.

Myth #4: As Long as I Have Something Valuable to Say, It Doesn't Matter How I Say It

I attended a presentation in southern California last year. The speaker was a well-known expert on his subject and had a great story to tell. The information was invaluable and I was excited to hear him speak.

He showed up in baggy pants that required him to constantly pull them up throughout his presentation. He fumbled with the video equipment the entire time and was unsure how to use it. He spent a tremendous amount of time making one point and never got to some of his more important points.

He had some very valuable information to share, but much of his credibility was lost in the presentation of the information. His mannerisms were very distracting and his material was extremely unorganized.

He struggled to relate the purpose of the information to the audience members, losing the practicality of the message. Most people walked out of the presentation wondering how to apply this information to their lives.

I have sat through more presentations than I care to count that emulate this scenario. I have read some outstanding books with information that has changed the course of my life. There have been times when I have traveled to hear the author speak and was sadly disappointed. The author was unable to make the transition from the pages of a book to the life of an audience.

Having valuable information is not enough to impact an audience. If it were, you could simply walk into a room, provide them with handouts of valuable information and let everyone go home. A good speaker learns the skill of taking valuable information and communicating it in a clear, concise, and articulate manner. Additionally, a good speaker will move the audience to action through the presentation.

We will look at ways to accomplish this in later sections. Just remember, having the information is just the first step. You must also master the skill of imparting that information to the audience in a way that instills value, applicability, and meaning.

If you don't plan to connect with the audience and inspire them to action, you may as well give them a handout and let them go home. The audience wants a speaker who is more personable and engaging than a handout.

Myth #5: As Long as I Say Something with Style, the Content is Not Important

I attended a financial planning conference many years ago. I don't recall the name of this particular session that I attended, but I will never forget the speaker. He was hysterical. He told funny stories and had us laughing the entire time. He was very entertaining and I truly enjoyed myself. There was just one problem. I didn't learn anything. I couldn't find the point to his presentation.

That's not really a problem when you go to a stand-up comedy show. In fact, the entire point is to make you laugh and entertain you. When you attend a business conference and you are paying to learn new ideas, tools, and techniques, you usually expect to learn something.

There's no rule that says you can't laugh hysterically and still learn a lot. In fact, humor is a great brain stimulator for learning, and I am all for it. I think this particular speaker had a real knack for humor, and with a message of substance, he could have knocked our socks off.

Had he just spent some time in preparation and development of his material, he could have imparted a few key points. We would have felt a tremendous amount of value in the presentation. Instead, we left feeling that his presentation was very entertaining, but somewhat void of meaning.

Just because you are an entertaining speaker doesn't mean you don't need to have a point. If you are hired or asked to give a presentation for the sole purpose of entertaining others, then it's not an issue.

However, if you are asked to give a business presentation and you spend the entire time entertaining everyone, you may have a problem with audience satisfaction. Most people will expect there to be a point somewhere in your presentation. A great speaker will learn to balance high content with high entertainment to give people some valuable content and information to walk away with, while at the same time allowing them to have fun in the process.

Myth #6: I'm Comfortable in Front of People, so I'll Make a Great Public Speaker

I was at a conference about a year ago and was sitting in the lobby. I was talking to a group of people and one of the men asked me what I did for a living. I told him I was a professional speaker. He proceeded to tell me how easy it was to get up in front of people and how comfortable he was talking in groups. He went on to say how he couldn't understand why people were afraid of it. He considered himself a ham and didn't have a problem giving presentations. He let me know he was teaching a class at the conference and asked me to stop by and say, "Hi."

I sat in his class and he was right. He had no fear whatsoever. He was very comfortable and at ease. And he stunk as a public speaker. He made stupid jokes and leaned on the lectern the entire time. His presentation had no structure or flow to it. His thoughts were random, spontaneous, and scattered. He was funny now and then, but he thought he was much funnier than he actually was.

When the class was over, he approached me and said, "See? It's not that difficult. You just get up there and do it. Just be yourself!"

"Well, you certainly have no fear. You were right about that." I smiled and slipped away before I had to be brutally honest with him.

Just because you're not afraid of something doesn't make you good at it. I'm not afraid of playing the violin, but I don't think you would want to be subjected to me jumping on a stage and playing for an hour without mastering the skill at some level. I have met quite a few people who have no fear of public speaking or getting up in front of people. As a result, they assume they have mastered the art of public speaking. Since most people associate fear with public speaking, those who are fearless consider themselves pros if they can speak in front of people without being nervous.

There is a lot more to giving a great presentation than being fearless. While the absence of fear will allow you to be more comfortable, you are still going to have to employ some basic techniques if you hope to provide your audience with some value. We will look at ways to structure a presentation to accomplish this goal in a later section.

Perceiving the Truth

Once you weed through all of the myths about public speaking, you can begin to perceive the reality and truth of it all. Giving butt kicking presentations is a skill that can be learned. It takes time, patience, and practice. Good speakers still experience nervousness, and even the best speakers have room for improvement.

5

THE BASICS OF A GREAT PRESENTATION

"We know that words cannot move mountains,
but they can move the multitude..."
—*Eric Hoffer*

There are a few key attributes to giving butt kicking presentations. Putting the presentation together is one step. Delivering it is a different step that requires adequate preparation. The delivery of the presentation will be discussed in a later section. This section will discuss the development of the presentation.

The first step in developing a speech or presentation is to have a point. What is the point of your presentation? You should be able to sit down and write out the purpose of your presentation in one sentence.

"If you can't write your message in a sentence,
you can't say it in an hour."
—*Dianna Booher*

Your objective should be very clear. Your presentation should have a few main points. Having too many points will overwhelm your audience. The length of your presentation will dictate how much you can elaborate on each point.

Once you have established your objective and formulated your main points, you are ready to develop a structured presentation. Your presentation should include:

- An introduction
- A main body
- A conclusion

The Speech Introduction

Every good speech or presentation needs a strong introduction. You must grab the attention of your audience right away and let them know that what you have to say is worth hearing. Your introduction should tell the audience what the purpose of your presentation is.

There are a number of techniques that can be used to spice up an introduction. Some speakers and presenters may use one or more of these tools:

- Famous quotes
- Humorous anecdotes
- Startling statistics
- Thought-provoking rhetorical questions
- Personal stories or illustrations
- Magic tricks
- Unique props
- Outrageous demonstrations

Regardless of the tool or technique that is used, it should be pertinent to the audience and the topic. Opening a speech with a famous quote is pointless if the quote does not relate to the main objective of the speech. Telling a humorous story just for the sake of "breaking the ice" is not a useful introduction tool.

The introduction of your speech may also be the time you let the audience know any special requests you might have. For example, when I present all-day training workshops, I let the attendees know right away that we will break every hour, so I request that people not leave the room in between unless it is absolutely necessary. Some speakers use this time to request that all questions be held until the end or that all cell phones and PDAs be set to the silent mode.

The venue of your speaking event will dictate how your introduction flows. A longer presentation allows for more "housekeeping" in the introduction (when the breaks are, where the bathrooms are located, etc). Training seminars are a good example of this. If you were giving a thirty minute speech to a Rotary Club, you would not need to address issues like this. When your time is limited, you need to utilize your introduction to really capture the attention of your audience.

Your introduction should be memorized. This is not a part of your presentation where you would want to "wing it." You should be very familiar with your introduction and it should flow smoothly.

Your audience will form an opinion of you within the first two minutes of your speech or presentation. Your introduction is very important. It should let your audience know that you have passion and conviction about your subject and you are excited to share the information with the audience.

The Main Body

This is the portion of your presentation where you develop your main points. The amount of time you are allotted for your presentation will help determine your number of points. You would not want to squeeze ten points into a thirty minute presentation.

Even if you are scheduled to do a longer presentation, you should still have a limited number of points. Anywhere from three to seven points would be adequate. Some examples of using points for your main body include:

- Five tips for successful selling

- Six main reasons people fail financially

- Seven steps to wise time management

- Four ways to cope with your teenager

- Three good reasons to watch your diet

- Five ways to increase your productivity

When you use points, steps, tips, etc., you create a structured flow in your presentation that is easy to follow. It's easy for your audience to follow, and it's easy for you to follow. If you do use points, you need to be sure you balance the time spent on each point.

I attended a presentation where the speaker spent forty-five minutes on the first point, and only fifteen minutes on the remaining four points. The presentation felt rushed after the first point. The speaker failed to prepare properly and did not manage her time throughout the presentation.

The main body of your presentation is the time to bring out your supporting facts and information to validate your objective. Props and visual aids can be used to further convey your point (we will explore these in more detail in a later section).

A central theme should be flowing throughout the main body of your presentation. Your audience should be able to follow a logical and structured line of thinking. As a speaker, you want to avoid going off on tangents while working your way through the main body of your speech. Stick to the main point (or points). Just remember, you are taking your audience on a journey to your main objective. Most audience members prefer to stay on the main road during the journey and not end up detoured on a bunch of rabbit trails. That doesn't mean you shouldn't add a lot of variety and unexpected turns—it simply means you should stick with the theme.

Some speakers often detour on their points and take the audience in a completely different direction that is irrelevant to the main objective of the presentation. As a result, the audience gets confused and frustrated. I have seen speakers do this, and they often get so engrossed in a "side story," that they forget what their point was.

Transitions

The main body of your presentation will include transitions from one point to the next. This is a great opportunity for you to spark the attention of the audience as you make a transition. You have an opportunity to do a number of things while you transition:

- Use a visual aid in your transition

- Use a point of humor to transition

- Incorporate a prop for the transition

- Vary your tone or volume as you transition

- Change your position in the room/on the stage

- Ask for questions on the previous point before transitioning

- Provide a handout as part of the transition

Transitions should be used as an opportunity to add some excitement, interest, and spark to your presentation. Otherwise, if you simply move methodically from one point to another without adding some pizzazz to your presentation, you will lull your audience to sleep. If your audience is a room full of hyperactive kindergarten kids strung out on sugar, then this may not be all bad. However, if your audience is a group of adults who have to endure a long presentation, you may want to add some variety to your transitions.

The ACID Test

When developing the main body of your speech, you want it to pass the ACID Test:

A—Attract Attention
C—Create Curiosity
I—Invoke Interest
D—Develop Desire

(Adapted from the IFSTA 5th edition Fire Service Instructor)

Your introduction and transitions are a great opportunity to attract attention. The title of your speech or presentation should also grab the attention of your audience. It should be something intriguing or even controversial (people love controversy!). Throughout the body of your speech, you can maintain the attention of your audience through props, visual aids, stories, humor, etc.

How do you create curiosity? One way to do this is by putting bits and pieces of information out to the audience that they are unfamiliar with. People want you to teach them something new. Tell them a little known fact relevant to the topic. This creates a sense of curiosity for more. Thought-provoking questions may also create curiosity as the audience contemplates the question.

You can invoke interest in your audience by telling them how your information will benefit them directly. People want to know how the information or speech applies to their lives. Some of the thoughts that occupy the minds of your attendees include:

- How is this going to benefit me?

- How can I put this information to use in my workplace?

- How can I use this information in my personal life?

- What new facts and information can I gain from this presentation?

- Is this going to be worth my time?

These are some of the main areas of interest for your audience. If you want to invoke interest, make sure you address some of these questions in your presentation. An example might be: "Next I am going to show you how to double your income in the next six months."

You now have the attention of every person in the room. You have also succeeded in creating a stimulating transition! Transitions are a great place to invoke interest during the main body of your presentation.

If you hope to develop desire, you really need to move people to action. You must give them a reason to really act on the message you have imparted. People will have a desire to embrace your message if you have clearly established the benefits of doing so.

The Conclusion

There is the well-known saying, "You never get a second chance to make a first impression." This is true, but there is also the saying, "Your last impression is the lasting impression." This is true as well. The close of your presentation is what will leave a lasting impression with your audience. You want to leave the audience with a strong impact.

Before we look at what to do when closing, let's talk about what *not* to do. No matter how great your presentation was, a weak and apathetic close will really hurt the effectiveness of your speech. I sat through a long presentation one afternoon, and it was full of great information. As the speaker began to wrap it up, he wasn't quite sure how to end it. His final words ended up something like this:

"Well, I think that's about it. I don't really have anything else to say on the topic. Thanks for listening for so long. I know you had better things to do today. I should have ended sooner. Okay, well I guess I'll shut up now before you throw tomatoes." He ended with a strained chuckle and sat down.

I started to wonder if maybe his presentation *was* too long. I began to realize I *did* have better things to do and I wasted a lot of time sitting in that room. He planted quite a few thoughts in my head that I hadn't thought of before. He had an opportunity to leave us with a powerful close and he missed it.

There's another common mistake that many speakers make when they close: they exceed their time allotment. If you are scheduled to speak for sixty minutes, speak for fifty five and wrap it up! No one ever got perturbed at a speaker for ending five minutes early but there have been *many* people who have been angered by a speaker who ends just five minutes late.

Unfortunately, I have endured many speakers who have gone over by fifteen to thirty minutes! The speaker failed to notice people looking at their watches. As the time dragged on, the speaker failed to notice people putting the watch up to their ear to see if it had stopped! The speaker missed all the signals: people gathering their items together, shifting in their seats, getting up and leaving the room, etc.

I have also endured many speakers who say, "In closing…" and then continue on and on for another twenty minutes. If you ever use the phrase, "In closing," or "In summary," or any other indication that you are wrapping it up, don't take more than two minutes to finish. When you use those phrases, you place anticipation in the minds of the audience that the presentation is coming to a close. Don't abuse their level of patience, and wrap it up.

No matter how great your presentation is, if you drag over your time allotment, you have left the audience with a bad impression. You have irritated many members of the audience, no matter how big or small the group. This rule applies in meetings, banquets, training seminars, keynote addresses, and any other speaking engagement you might have. End on time. I can't stress this enough:

Never, NEVER, EVER go over time!

Lengthy presentations or training seminars usually require that you summarize your main points before you close. This helps to tie everything together before you wrap up with your close. Maybe you've heard the saying "Tell them what you're going to tell them. Then tell them. Then tell them what you told them." Wrapping up gives you the opportunity to summarize and tell then what you've told them.

The Powerful Close

This is your opportunity to really leave the audience with something to think about. You should never be "winging" your close. You should have a memorized, powerful close that leaves an indelible mark on your audience.

You want the close of your presentation to have power and impact. There are a number of ways to accomplish this:

- Leave them laughing with a humorous close

- Close with a magic trick that relates to your presentation

- Use a famous quote to end your presentation with a strong close

- Tell a touching or inspirational story

- Issue a challenge or appeal

- Move the audience to action

- Close with an outrageous demonstration

- Use a surprising or shocking story

Humor is a great way to end a speech, but should be used with caution. There is an entire section of this book dedicated to the use of humor in presentations. When using humor to close, make sure it is relevant to the presentation and has a point. You don't want to leave your audience with the feeling that you're being flippant. I watched one presenter close a presentation with this: "Now I would like to close by telling you a joke." She proceeded to tell a very off color, classless joke that diminished the credibility of her entire presentation. Don't be that person.

Never underestimate the importance of your closing. Some of the best speeches in the world have powerful closes that people have never forgotten. Here are some powerful closes from some famous speeches:

Finally, whether you are citizens of America or citizens of the world, ask of us here the same high standards of strength and sacrifice which we ask of you. With a good conscience our only sure reward, with history the final judge of our deeds, let us go forth to lead the land we love, asking His blessing and His help, but knowing that here on earth God's work must truly be our own. *(President John F. Kennedy, Inaugural Address, January 20, 1961)*

With malice toward none; with charity for all; with firmness in the right, as God gives us to see the right, let us strive on to finish the work we are in; to bind up the nation's wounds; to care for him who shall have borne the battle, and for his widow, and his orphan—to do all which may achieve and cherish a just and lasting peace, among ourselves, and with all nations. *(Abraham Lincoln, Second Inaugural Address Washington, D.C. March 4, 1865)*

The crew of the Space Shuttle Challenger honored us by the manner in which they lived their lives. We will never forget them, nor the last time we saw them, this morning, as they prepared for the journey and waved goodbye and slipped the surly bonds of earth to touch the face of God. *(Ronald Reagan, Speech on the Challenger Disaster, January 28, 1986)*

Let us build wisely, let us build surely, let us build faithfully, let us build not for the moment, but for the years that are to come, and so establish here below what we hope to find above - a house of many mansions, where there shall be room for all. *(Winston Churchill, Speech at Kinnaird Hall, Dundee on May 4, 1908)*

Free at last! Free at last! Thank God Almighty, we are free at last! *(Martin Luther King—I have a Dream)*

A good closing will always leave your audience with something to think about. An inspirational story with a solid moral or an unexpected ending is very effective. A magic trick that ties in your topic and dumbfounds the audience is another technique. Quoting famous authors or speakers can also provide a great close.

Whatever you choose to close your presentation, make sure you have memorized it and practiced it over and over. You want it to come across smoothly. If you spend some time and energy on your close, you will leave your audience with something powerful to remember you by.

6

TYPES OF PRESENTATIONS

"The right to be heard does not automatically include the right to be taken seriously."
—*Hubert H. Humphrey*

There are a variety of speech types for a variety of purposes. You wouldn't want to give an informative speech during a toast at a wedding! You wouldn't want to give an impromptu speech at an annual board of directors meeting. There are different speech types that fit certain occasions better than others. Below is an explanation of the basic types of speeches that exist.

Formal Speeches

A formal speech is usually memorized or typed out and referenced as the speaker is presenting. Normally, people giving formal speeches are not attempting to "wing it," or think on their feet. They tend to have more of a somber disposition versus a jovial approach to the speech. If it is a long formal speech, you will usually find someone behind a lectern referencing speech notes. The person may even have the entire speech typed out in front of them.

If you ever have to give a formal speech, it's perfectly acceptable to have lots of notes or even have the speech typed out. However, you should never be so dependent on the notes that you cannot make eye contact with your audience or look up from your notes. You should still be very familiar with the flow of your speech and have a general idea of what you will be saying. When giving a formal speech, it's also acceptable to interject humor and lighten the mood if the humor is appropriate and relevant.

A formal speech requires a certain level of polish. The speaker needs to speak clearly and present gracefully. Since you are normally behind a lectern and can use notes in a formal speech, you have the opportunity to eliminate all "ah's," "um's," and other filler words that people often use when trying to find a thought.

Have you ever watched politicians give a formal speech versus an impromptu interview? In a formal speech, they sound eloquent, prepared, and polished. They know what they are going to say and how they will say it. They have the speech in front of them or a teleprompter that guides them through the speech. When you watch them in a debate or an interview, you will often see them stumble on their words or use "uh" and "um" over and over as they annoy the listeners. Mastering the formal speech is much easier than mastering the art of public speaking as a whole.

When giving a formal speech, it is best to limit the amount of time you speak. Formal speeches are not usually animated and lack some of the props and demonstrations that keep the audience lively and awake. Formal speeches are usually appropriate for formal events or events that call for a prepared speech. Some examples of appropriate occasions for formal speeches include:

- Wedding toasts

- Funerals

- Accepting and presenting awards

- Retirement celebrations

- Formal dinners

- Political speeches

- Annual corporate meetings

Informative Speeches

There are a variety of informative speeches. The purpose of an informative speech is to provide information to your audience about a particular subject. Informative speeches may describe, explain, or demonstrate the point of the speaker. When giving an informative speech, you should consider the five W's and the How:

- Who?

- What?

- When?

- Where?

- Why?

- How?

Let's assume you are going to give an informative talk to an audience about the risks of heart disease. You would need to address the questions on the previous page.

Who are you talking about? Who is more at risk than others? Who should be especially cognizant of diet and exercise?

What is heart disease? What can be done to prevent it? What are the most common contributors?

When is heart disease most likely to strike? When should you start thinking about heart disease?

Where can your audience go to take action? Where can they get more information?

Why does heart disease exist? Why is this information important? Why should your audience act on it?

How does your information apply to each person in the room? How does it help? How can it be used in everyday life? How can every person avoid the risks of heart disease?

Informative speeches can be longer in length if they are broken up with interactivity, demonstrations, or props. Using visual aids in informative speeches helps your audience to grasp the information. The amount of time you have available to give an informative speech will dictate how many visual aids or props you can incorporate into your presentation. Informative speeches are best used for the following purposes:

- Seminars

- Informal meetings

- Informational meetings

- Workshops

- Informational briefings

- Conferences and conventions

Let me make it clear that informative does not need to be synonymous with boring. Many speakers who are tasked with giving informative presentations on a regular basis complain that people just think the information is dull. Well I have news for you: there is no such thing as a boring topic—there are only boring presenters!

Entertaining Speeches

Everyone loves to be entertained! That's why the entertainment industry is so lucrative. We spend copious amounts of money on movies, vacations, amusement parks, and everything we can think of that entertains us.

The purpose of the entertaining speech is to provide a form of diversion. The goal is to get the audience focused and thinking about something other than the stress in their lives.

Entertaining an audience is not always an easy task, especially if it has been established that the sole purpose of your speech is to entertain. There's a little bit of pressure there! Normally, speakers incorporate entertainment into other types of speeches like a motivational speech.

Many people think that if your goal is to entertain an audience, you will have to make them laugh and you have to be funny. People are entertained by a variety of topics, as evidenced by the variety of movies that entertain people. Some are funny, some are serious, and some are action-packed. An audience is easily entertained by great stories, personal experiences, and special interests, whether funny or serious.

Using magic and juggling can be very entertaining. Dramatic talks can be entertaining, as well as humorous personal stories. Some speakers sing and dance during entertaining speeches. That's not my thing, but more power to them!

There is a term in the speaking world called "Edutainment." It refers to entertaining people while you educate them. I do a lot of informative presentations via training workshops and seminars. I always try to incorporate some form of entertainment to keep the class lively. Sometimes I use magic tricks or card tricks. Other times I tell stories or add funny anecdotes to provide some diversion. There are times when I juggle to depict a specific point. Other times I provide activities for the attendees to participate in. Incorporating some form of entertainment into many of your presentations will help keep them lively.

A strictly entertaining speech does not aim to educate people or persuade them to any particular action. The entertaining speech is usually designed for the sole purpose of entertaining the listeners. Some examples of appropriate venues for entertaining speeches include:

- After dinner speeches

- Roasts

- Keynote speeches

- Social club events

- Conferences and conventions

Motivational and Inspirational Speeches

Motivational speakers are in high-demand as people want to be "pumped up" in their jobs and personal lives. Motivational talks provide people with some excitement and incentive for improving their lives. Many motivational speakers also educate and inform the audience. Some provide tools and techniques that can be used to improve a variety of areas in life. Some of the topics that motivational speakers often focus on are:

- Personal improvement

- Increasing sales

- Customer service

- Excelling in work

- Excelling in life

Inspirational speakers might focus on simply inspiring the audience to strive for excellence in life. Many inspirational speakers share personal stories about triumph and victory. Maybe the speaker has overcome a huge obstacle in life and is now an inspiration to others. Maybe the speaker has failed miserably in one area and has used the failure to reach success in another area. This type of speech would inspire others to keep trying after failure. Many speeches contain elements of both a motivational speech and an inspirational speech.

Some of the best speeches I have ever heard have been motivational and inspirational speeches. When a speaker becomes vulnerable enough to share a deep personal experience that can inspire others, there is a connection that is made with the audience. Motivational and inspirational speeches can take on a variety of tones:

- Humorous

- Serious

- Shocking

- Moving

- Suspenseful

- Unexpected

Truly motivational and inspirational speeches draw large crowds. People love to be motivated and inspired. There is just a great feeling you have in the pit of your stomach when you walk away from a well-done motivational or inspirational speech.

Speakers that attempt to deliver a motivational speech are usually animated or full of energy. They are able to spread the excitement about a particular subject. They move the audience to laughter and tears. The audience leans forward to glean more. Everyone loves a great motivational speaker. Some examples of appropriate venues for motivational and inspirational speeches include:

- Keynote speeches

- Special events

- Conferences and conventions

- Annual corporate meetings

- Political addresses

- Church events

- Family and couple retreats

Persuasive Speeches

The purpose of a persuasive speech is to persuade the audience or listener to your point of view. You may be attempting to sway a group to take action on a noble cause. Maybe you are in a sales position and need to persuade people every day. Perhaps your job requires artful negotiations that would be enhanced with persuasive speaking skills.

I have listened to many persuasive speeches in my life: speeches for gun control and speeches against it; speeches for and against war; speeches attempting to convince listeners to invest in a time-share property; speeches for and against abortion; speeches by organizational leaders trying to move the masses in the direction of the vision of the organization; and the list goes on.

Persuasive speakers use a variety of tools in their speeches. They may use emotion to persuade the audience as they tug on their heart strings. They may use startling statistics to change a point of view. Speakers may incorporate demonstrations to drive their point home. They may incorporate some elements of the motivational speech to persuade their listeners. Photographs, charts, and visual displays may be used to persuade listeners.

Persuasive speakers often provide a tremendous amount of fact to drive their point home. Strong language and vivid words are often used to move people to the speaker's position. The speaker will take into consideration the audience and their views. The speaker needs to know how difficult it will be to sway opinion, and what percentage of support already exists.

Pulling off a persuasive speech takes a certain level of confidence and charisma. Some examples of appropriate venues for persuasive speeches include:

- Activist or political speeches

- Stockholder meetings

- Debates

- Cold calling

- Time-share presentations

- Sales training

Impromptu Speeches

There are times when we are expected to speak off the cuff. Maybe we are asked to stand up in a meeting and explain a concept or clarify a point. There may be times when we are called up to the stage to accept an award. Perhaps we are put on the spot to give our opinion on a particular topic. Maybe we are engaged in a debate and we don't know what questions to expect.

Impromptu speaking is essentially any speaking that we are not adequately prepared for. Offering a question and answer time at the end of any other type of speech will require some impromptu skills.

If you want to observe impromptu speakers, just tune in to some of the nightly news shows. Many of these programs will have guest speakers who appear on their show. As they exchange questions, answers, and heated debate, you can see how different people perform under impromptu conditions.

Some speakers think very well on their feet and are able to articulate their thoughts quickly and concisely. Others are downright painful to listen to and watch! Their sentences are flooded with "um's," and "ah's," and you're just dying to help them find their words and finish their sentences.

Can you actually practice your impromptu skills and improve? Absolutely. Nearly all of your speaking throughout the day is impromptu. When you answer the phone, you certainly don't have a prepared speech as you respond to questions. When you are approached at work and asked to explain something, you tap into your impromptu skills.

The best way to improve in this area is to become aware of how you speak. The next time you are engaged in a conversation, notice how you formulate your thoughts. Do you allow moments of silence while you search for words, or do you fill the silence with "ah's" and "um's"? Do you look up or down when searching for words, or are you able to maintain eye contact with your listener? Do you have a habit of repeating words or phrases? Do you fidget when you talk or are you able to maintain concentration?

Impromptu speaking requires an awareness of your common speaking habits. Some people scratch their noses. Some fidget with their hands. Some constantly push their glasses up on their nose. Others jingle change in their pocket. If you want to know what your quirks are, ask people who listen to you talk all the time. The people closest to me are the ones who cured me of my bad habits when speaking off the cuff. I had a habit of clicking a pen and saying "um" when trying to find my words. I also scratched the back of my neck occasionally just as a self-conscious habit. It didn't itch, and I wasn't aware I did it. Once it was pointed out, I became aware of it and stopped.

You will engage in impromptu speaking more than any other style of speaking. Thinking on your feet is something you have to do every day. Some examples of where you can expect to give impromptu speeches include:

- Meetings

- Awards ceremonies

- Special events

- Debates

- Teleconferences

- Social events

- Question and answer sessions

- Everyday conversations

High Tech Presentations

There are several types of high tech presentations where you may be giving a seminar or presenting valuable information. These types of presentations include:

- Webinars (Webcasts)

- Podcasts

- Video Conferencing

- Social Networking

Webinars and Webcasts

Webinars and webcasts are Internet-driven workshops or presentations. Face-to-face presentations are always the most effective tool for teaching, motivating, or inspiring audiences. However, webinars and webcasts fill a need for organizations that can't afford to send all of their employees to certain training classes. These tools are also beneficial for people (presenters and attendees) who can't travel very often.

There are a few tips you may find useful when conducting webinars or webcasts. Your topic description is what will get people to register, so make it interesting. Your presentation is what will get people to stick around for the entire presentation, so *be* interesting! With in-person presentations, people feel more obligated to not get up and leave in the middle of your presentation for fear they may appear rude. With a webinar or webcast, they don't care. They will leave the room very quickly if your presentation is dull.

If you are using sound and speaking while presenting, you need to use more voice fluctuation and incorporate some stories and humor. Some presenters find this difficult because there is no audience feedback with laughter or facial expressions. It takes a little practice to deliver like a pro in a web presentation, so give it some time.

If you are not using sound in a webinar or webcast, you need to use lots of graphics and make it as interactive as possible. Funny videos and humorous pictures are always a big hit. Just keep reminding yourself of what I said earlier: there is no such thing as a boring topic—there are only boring presenters!

You can also utilize "chat" technology with your web presentation to keep it more interactive. This allows the attendees to ask questions either throughout the presentation or at a designated time. When answering questions via the chat mode, resist the temptation to slip into your "text language" where you abbreviate everything and shorten words. You need to remain professional and type everything correctly. I know this takes a little longer, but if you spend enough time at the keyboard, you will become a whiz at it.

Podcasts

Podcasts got their names from "broadcast" and "iPod." They are audio or video files that can be downloaded to an iPod or any MP3 player. They can also be broadcast over the Internet. Podcasts have become a popular way for people to listen to talk radio shows, news, music, informational speakers, motivational presenters, etc. One of the things that has made Podcasts so popular is the ability to set your computer to automatically download your favorite Podcasts and then automatically sync to your MP3 player.

If you want people to download and listen to your Podcast, you need to be compelling, interesting, or entertaining. As with all presentations, rattling off boring but useful information will not retain the attention of the listener. Being passionate in a Podcast is extremely helpful. Having new and fresh information is important if you want to reach the Podcast audience. Having a new Podcast every day, or once a week, or at any regular interval will keep people coming back for more (as long as it is compelling, interesting, or entertaining).

Video Conferencing

When I was a young child, I caught a few episodes of Star Trek. I was amazed at the concept of being able to talk to someone in real time while watching them on a monitor. Of course it was unheard of back then (cell phones weren't even around!). Now video phones and video conferencing is making it possible to conduct meetings and presentations without leaving your office or home (but please... still shower and comb your hair for crying out loud!).

Video conferencing and video phones send sound and picture from a microphone and camera over the Internet or a phone line. Webcams are now built into laptop and desktop computers, making it possible to communicate with people across the globe who also have a webcam. Skype is one service available that allows you to download software and allows you to talk, chat, or video call for free from your computer as long as the other person downloads the software as well.

If you use PowerPoint, it can be viewed by all attendees at the same time, creating a similar atmosphere as face-to-face. Virtual whiteboards can also be used which allows for brainstorming and input from people in different locations who are participating in the video conference. Current technology is also making it possible for all attendees to have access to what is being viewed on a computer screen and even make changes to documents on that computer during the video conference which can facilitate more collaboration.

The same guidelines for all presentation types apply to video conferencing. The tendency with video conferencing is for people to get too casual and lose some of the professional elements of an in-person presentation. Try to maintain the same level of professionalism in a video conference as a face-to-face presentation. Additionally, true eye contact is lost in group video conferencing, which would normally allow the presenter to connect with the audience. Keeping the energy level high is more challenging with video conferencing than face-to-face. As a result, you as the presenter need to bring some extra energy to the table (or the video screen).

Social Networking

Many presenters, business executives, salespeople, etc. are turning to social networking to get their message out. Social networking includes Facebook, MySpace, LinkedIn, blogging, Twitter, and every other fad phase that hits the Internet. I am all for keeping up with this stuff, but I think you can take it too far and spend way too much time on these social networking sites and too little time improving your presentation skills.

As you utilize these tools, consider moderation. Needing to be updated or needing to update people ten times a day is overkill. People become numb to it and start to ignore your posts and messages. This applies to Ezines (electronic magazines and newsletters) and email updates as well. If I get more than two automated emails a month from anyone, they go straight into the trash. When I only get something once a month or once in awhile, my interest is peaked and I will take a look at it. Be careful not to use technology to scare people away from your message.

Presentations can include a variety of the different types of speeches above. You may have an informative seminar that includes entertainment. You may have a motivational speech that is also persuasive. An impromptu speech may end up informing the audience or inspiring them. A high tech presentation may include several other types of speeches.

Regardless of the style of speech you choose, all styles should still contain the basic elements of a speech as discussed in the previous section. Even an impromptu presentation should contain an introduction, a main body, and a conclusion. Listeners should always be able to follow the flow of a speech, regardless of the type of speech you choose.

Some speakers excel in one particular style of speaking while others may do well with a few different styles. Speakers normally find a niche and stick with it. It is better to be outstanding at one thing than to be good at five things.

As you examine your own speaking style and the venues you will need to speak in, you can begin to pick and choose which style of speech will work best. You may find a combination of two or more styles that suit you well.

7

COPING WITH THE PRE-SPEAKING JITTERS

"Fear makes the wolf bigger than he is."
—*German Proverb*

I made the mistake of standing behind the door and peering into the room as the attendees were finding their seats. I could feel my heart beating and I was starting to sweat. I only had five more minutes before I had to walk out from behind that door and start talking. Everyone would be looking at me. Everyone would expect me to have something to say that was worth their time and money.

I was about to teach my first set of financial planning seminars. People had been checking in at the registration desk and I was hiding in a back room trying to "prepare myself." I was attempting to control my nervousness and get a grip on myself. It wasn't working. The main reason it wasn't working was because I was allowing myself to *obsess*.

All I could think about was how nervous I was. I took deep breaths. That didn't work. I just ended up light-headed. I peeked out at the crowd again and tried to picture them all in their underwear. That didn't work. I was really feeling sick now! I picked up a cup of water to drink and I could see my hand shaking. This was not good.

My five minutes was up and I had to step into the room and begin speaking. It was a sorry opening, but after about five minutes, I finally gained some control over my nerves. I started to relax and focus more on my presentation than on myself. After about fifteen minutes, I was much more at ease.

It took me a long time to learn how to master the pre-speaking jitters that were once pre-speaking panic attacks. I still get small jitters every once in awhile, but I have established some routines through the years that have really helped me to get over that anxiety. Some sure signs of pre-speaking jitters include:

- Cotton mouth

- Excessive sweat

- Trembling hands and legs

- Nausea

- Anxiety

- Rapid pulse rate

- Twitching eyes

- Blurred vision

- Headache

- Tight throat

- Shaky or squeaky voice

I have experienced every single one of these at some time or another. I can remember the first presentation I ever gave, and I experienced all of them at once! It was like an uncontrollable wave of anxiety, and I had no idea what to do about it. It was ugly… I wouldn't wish that on any audience. There are some basic steps you can take before you speak to help with nervousness before the presentation:

- Be completely prepared long before you have to speak

- Don't put anything off until the last minute

- Know your material (just before you speak is not the time to practice)

- Have the beginning of your presentation memorized so it flows smoothly.

- Have all equipment set up and tested at least thirty minutes before you speak (all audio and visual equipment)

- Don't go off into a room by yourself and obsess

- Stretch your legs, neck, and back

- Get out and mingle with the people you will be speaking to. You will become more comfortable with them and they won't seem like strangers to you.

- Find out the names of people in your audience

- Listen to conversations and pick up funny things you can bring up in your presentation

- Look around the room and find humorous things you can talk about

- Preoccupy yourself with talking to people instead of focusing on your nervousness

- Don't eat a big meal before you speak (your stomach may cramp from the stress)

- Don't drink caffeine. Your tendency is to talk fast when you're nervous. If you drink coffee, you will be talking 100 mph with gusts up to 200!

- Don't drink water if you have cotton mouth—the water washes away the saliva and doesn't help. Instead, eat a lemon drop which actually creates more saliva. It works. I do this all the time.

- If your throat is tight, yawn to relax the muscles

- Make a conscious effort to slow down your breathing

- Take one or two deep breaths to relax

Try to remember that a little bit of nervousness is actually beneficial. It will get your adrenaline pumping and push you to perform better if you allow it to. If you use your nervousness as a positive source of energy, you will appear more vivacious and enthusiastic about your topic. You will have more energy and the audience will pick up on that. There is nothing more grueling than having to sit through a lethargic, apathetic presentation. Use the pre-speaking jitters to liven up your delivery.

Often times, you will experience a small surge of anxiety when you first step onto the stage or in front of the audience.

Just remember that your initial anxiety will subside as you begin to focus more on your presentation and focus less on yourself. This takes time, so be patient with yourself. Here are some techniques to assist you with your nervousness while you are speaking:

- Don't draw attention to your nervousness—it's not as obvious as you might think it is. You feel much more nervous than you look, I can assure you.

- Don't apologize for your presentation—it makes the audience quiet and uncomfortable as they shift in their seats. This will only add to your nervousness.

- If you have trembling hands, don't hold anything in your hands, especially a cup of water. The audience will watch it shake all the way to your mouth! If you need notes, place them on a lectern where you can reference them, but don't hold them in your hands. Index cards work much better when you are nervous.

- If your legs are trembling, move around a little as you are talking. Take a few steps and then stop and address your audience. Don't pace! It really annoys people and it's distracting.

- Don't make eye contact with the grumpy faces in the audience at first. Instead, find the smiling, happy faces, and make eye contact with them. It will help you to relax. Just make sure you don't ignore the grumps for the rest of your presentation. Sometimes your smile and demeanor will lighten up theirs.

- Start to pour your energy into your presentation and don't think about everyone staring at you. As you get more into your topic, you will relax and shine!

Advance Preparation

I have given too many presentations where I was not adequately prepared. I often learned my lesson the hard way. I have started going through my PowerPoint slides and realized that the text transitions were not completed properly. I have given presentations where I was completely unprepared for some of the questions I would get. I have spoken to groups and not anticipated controversial topics that may arise. I have given a speech and fumbled over difficult phrases that I hadn't practiced out loud. All of these factors only add to nervousness.

There is no substitute for being prepared. If you know what to expect, your level of anxiety diminishes greatly. If you have planned in advance, even the unexpected events can be handled smoothly. There are some great ways to prepare well in advance for your presentation:

- Practice your presentation in front of a mirror. You can see what your gestures look like.

- Video tape your presentation in advance. Observe your nervous habits.

- Have someone you trust listen to your presentation and give you honest pointers

- Say your speech out loud so you can see if you stumble over any words or phrases

- Visualize your presentation and the successful delivery

- Visualize a smiling audience

- Know how the room will be set up and where people will be seated

- Don't put any part of the planning and preparing off until the last minute

- Visit the location where you will be speaking and get a feel for the room

- Ask for a lapel microphone instead of a hand-held in case your hands are shaking

- Go through every single slide of a PowerPoint presentation and double check all text transitions

- Make sure any visual aids are free of spelling errors and tie-pose (I mean typos!)

- Spend some time thinking about potential questions and answers on your topic

- Find out if the group has any controversial issues they are dealing with

- Find out if there are any people in the group who may have a "chip on their shoulder"

- Make a list of everything you need for your presentation. Look at the list before you leave. Take the list with you and reference it before you make your presentation.

  - Stay Positive!

Advance preparation for an extended workshop or seminar is much more extensive and will be covered in chapter 15, "Attention to Detail." When preparing for a short presentation, the majority of the focus should be on your material and the delivery. Continual practice and preparation will go a long way to ease uncertainty and nervousness.

"Spectacular achievement is always preceded by spectacular preparation."
—*Robert H. Schuller*

8

THE DELIVERY

*"Good communication is as stimulating as black coffee,
and just as hard to sleep after."*
—Anne Morrow Lindbergh

"People respond more to what they see than what they hear." I've heard this said in regards to public speaking, and I wasn't always sure I bought into this until I attended a well-publicized presentation. The speaker was a well-known author (I will leave out names to be nice), and was sure to draw a huge crowd. He already had a great reputation for the information in his books.

I paid a good chunk of money and drove two hours to hear him speak. I had read his books and was anxious to listen to his words of wisdom in person. I arrived early to get a good parking spot. I waited patiently for the program to start. A huge screen filled the front of the room with motivational sayings, beautiful pictures, and small doses of what we could expect. Motivational music was playing in the background and I was getting pumped up for this presentation!

A tall man in a sharp suit jogged out on to the stage and took the microphone. He gave a fantastic introduction of the speaker and we all applauded with great excitement. The speaker casually made his way to center stage and smiled. He took the microphone in one hand and slipped his other hand into his pocket.

He spent the next ten minutes talking about some of the material in one of his best books. He talked very slowly and methodically. He said "um" a lot and kept his hand in his pocket. He was without enthusiasm and his tone began to lull the audience into a sense of apathy. I looked around the room and watched as people shifted in their seats. This was not what we had expected.

The information he had to offer was already credible and valuable. He had proven that with his book sales. However, his delivery as a public speaker left much to be desired. He just wasn't connecting with the audience. As a result, I had a very difficult time responding to his words. I began to realize that people really do respond more to what they see than what they hear. What I saw was a terrible public speaker, and that deafened me to his real message. I ended up leaving forty minutes into his presentation. I noticed many other people leaving as well.

Delivery is imperative if you hope to give a good presentation. No matter how good your message is, it won't be received if your delivery stinks. Your delivery includes:

- **Your Introduction:** Your speech starts with how you are introduced. Never underestimate the power of a great introduction. You should always try to have someone else introduce you. Make sure the person who introduces you sets a positive tone for the audience and establishes you as an authority or expert on the topic. The introduction should let the audience know why they should pay attention to you. It should arouse their interest. The best way to ensure a great introduction is to write it yourself. Try to limit it to one or two short paragraphs. Type it out legibly and go over it with the person who will introduce you. Make sure they pronounce all words correctly, and don't be afraid to have that person practice the introduction with you. This will give you the opportunity to coach them on giving a great introduction.

- **Your Appearance:** How you dress is important. If you are speaking to a group of business executives and you show up in tattered jeans and a white t-shirt, you might have a challenge getting them to listen to your message. If your clothes are wrinkled or stained, that will distract from your message. If your hair is wild and messy, you will be hard-pressed to get people to take your words seriously. If you're doing a stand-up comedy routine, that could be to your advantage. However, if you're addressing a group of business executives on a serious topic, it may detract from your message.

- **Your Body Language:** Your gestures will convey apathy or excitement. If you stand completely still the entire time with your hands buried in your pockets, you will bore your audience. If you repeat the same annoying gesture over and over, you will irritate the audience. If you stand hunched over, you will not convey a sense of confidence. If you use your gestures to further convey your points and throw some energy into your presentation, your message will come across more emphatically. If you stand and walk with confidence, your audience will place more authoritative weight on your message. If you are tentative and unsure in your body language, your audience will question the credibility of your message.

- **Your Tone of Voice:** It is very difficult to sit and listen to a monotone speaker for any extended amount of time. Normally, this will lull you to sleep. The audience has a difficult time absorbing the message of an apathetic speaker. Tone of voice plays a very big role in your delivery. Changing volume and pitch adds variety to the presentation and the audience needs that variety.

Don't Annoy Your Audience

In the course of my years of speaking experience, I have conducted many surveys. I have asked thousands of people what annoys them most about speakers and presenters. These "annoying things" create barriers in the delivery of the message.

Once a speaker starts annoying the audience, they are no longer paying attention to the words, as they are focused on the delivery and the very thing that annoys them. The survey results have often left me laughing as I shake my head in disbelief. I just can't believe some of the things that audiences are subjected to in the course of training, seminars, conferences, meetings, and various other speaking events. Some of the ways speakers annoy their audience in the delivery include:

- Scratching body parts

- Playing with change in pocket

- Constantly looking at watch

- Leaning on lecterns with elbows

- Pacing like a caged animal

- Standing like a statue

- Repetitive gestures

- Speaking too slowly

- Speaking at top speed

- Constantly saying "ah" or "um"

- Repeating words or phrases over and over (like "you know" or "and so")

- Making a weak and apologetic introduction when the speaker first begins

- No sense of humor

- Monotone voice

- Not starting on time

- Eating while talking

- Chewing gum while speaking

- Inappropriate clothing

- Acting unprofessionally

- Cleaning wax out of ear with a key (yes, this actually happened!)

- Picking nose

- Blowing nose

- Speaking down to the audience

- Talking over the heads of the audience

- Using industry jargon that the audience doesn't understand

- Reading a speech word-for-word

- Talking to the screen with back to the audience

- Mumbling

- Not knowing how to use audio and visual equipment

- Not giving breaks in long presentations

- Using off-color jokes and humor

- Embarrassing people in the audience

- Being unorganized in delivery

- Not having a point

- Not getting to the point

- Going over the time limit

- Saying "In summary," or "In closing," and then going on and on and on

You can see that the list is long! There are a lot of things that speakers do to annoy the audience. If you are aware of what annoys people, you can stop doing it! I will cover a few of these items in more detail, as they seem to be common problems with many speakers.

Body Gestures
There are a lot of things that fall into this category. Pacing, standing still, and repetitive gestures should all be avoided.

People often struggle with what to do with their hands. They feel awkward just having their hands at their sides, so they stuff them in their pockets. Or they hold them clasped in front of them ("The Fig Leaf"). Or they hold them behind their back ("The Reverse Fig Leaf").

Some people hold their hands in front of them clasped together with just the pointer fingers up ("The Steeple"). Others bring their hands together in front of them with all five fingers of one hand touching the five fingers of the other hand. A common repetitive gesture is to assume this position of the hand and then pull the hands away from each other and toward each other repeatedly. It's really annoying and distracting, and a lot of speakers do it.

A common gesture for many speakers is pointing, and it's a bad habit. It can put members of the audience on the defensive, and that's not a good thing. You can gesture with your entire hand without having to point, and it is still effective.

So what should you do with your hands? You need to learn to feel comfortable leaving them at your sides unless you are gesturing. Any gestures should be a natural extension of you expressing yourself, and not something strained or distracting.

What about the rest of your body? Pacing, standing like a statue, and shifting weight to one hip is common. This can all be distracting. You should stand in one place with your feet shoulder width apart and your weight evenly distributed (without locking the knees). This is called the "grounded" position. You are firmly grounded and not leaning on anything.

When you move, take two to three steps and then resume your "grounded" position. This will keep you from pacing and subjecting your audience to motion sickness. If you are speaking to a very large audience with a large area to move around, you can take more steps before grounding yourself again. If you are in a small room with a small audience, you may end up staying primarily in one area and only taking minor steps now and then throughout the presentation.

Body gestures play a huge role in your delivery. You can use your gestures to make important points, add dramatization, add enthusiasm, and add variety. The key is allowing your gestures to come naturally and serve as an enhancement to your message, not a distraction.

Appearance

Your appearance will play a huge role in how the audience receives your message. I have sat through many presentations where I missed the whole message as a result of being distracted by the speaker's appearance.

In one seminar, the speaker had his tie tied too short. It barely dropped below his chest and looked ridiculous. To make matters worse, he wore a hideous, loud, checkered jacket that kept many of the audience members poking fun at him under their breath. I can't even remember what he talked about.

I listened to another speaker at a conference who wore these huge, dangling earrings that knocked her neck every time she moved. I could see the audience flinch when she moved from one side of the stage to the other. None of us were listening to her message because we were too fixated on her earrings!

I sat through another presentation that was downright painful to watch. The speaker was visibly nervous, and she wore a tan suit. Her arm pits were drenched in sweat, and every time she lifted her arm, I cringed. It was blatantly obvious and very distracting to the audience.

When considering what to wear to a speaking engagement, try to follow these guidelines:

- Avoid flashy jewelry

- Avoid flashy ties, scarves, or jackets

- Avoid clothes that are too tight or too loose

- Make sure your pants are not three inches too short—it looks dumb!

- If you are prone to sweating while speaking, wear dark colors

- Dress appropriately for your audience (not over-dressed or under-dressed)

Using the Microphone
If there is one area in which speakers really annoy their audience, it's with the microphone. I'll start with the hand-held microphone. There are a few simple guidelines to follow to ensure that you are not annoying your audience:

- **Hold the microphone under your chin.** The microphone should be held towards the center of your chest, a few inches under your chin (basically, the same area that a lapel microphone would be located). The microphone should be tested before speaking to ensure people in the back can hear everything. If the sound is not loud enough, don't pull the microphone closer to your mouth. Instead, turn up the sound volume. If you keep pulling the microphone closer to your mouth, you end up magnifying the sound of your breath and it creates an irritating feedback in the sound system. This annoys the audience, and I think we have established that annoying the audience is bad.

- **Keep the microphone under your mouth.** If you turn towards a screen to make a point and the microphone doesn't follow your mouth, your voice trails off and the audience can't hear you. Again, that annoys the audience. Anytime you move or turn your head, the microphone should follow to maintain a consistent level of sound.

- **Stay away from the sound speakers.** If you stand too close to the speakers, you will get a nasty hiss or squeal of feedback. This *really* annoys the audience, and they will let you know with painful grimaces and fingers in their ears. Keep the microphone clear of the speakers and you will avoid this feedback.

- **Move the microphone away from your mouth when making disgusting noises.** I had to sit and listen to a speaker during a question and answer session and he was driving everyone crazy! He kept making that gross sound that people make when trying to move fluids down from the nasal cavity to the throat. It wouldn't have been nearly as bad if he would have thought to move the microphone away from his mouth! ICK!

The lavaliere microphone is a pretty popular way to amplify a speaker. It allows the speaker to free up his/her hands for gestures or demonstrations. There are a few pointers to consider when using the lavaliere microphone:

- **Stay away from the speakers.** This rule is the same for all microphones. Stay clear of any equipment that will provide feedback.

- **Test the microphone in advance.** You don't want to be messing with it during a presentation. You should have the sound level set and have the receiver comfortably situated somewhere out of sight.

- **Know where the mute button is.** Again, if you need to clear your throat or make disgusting noises, do the audience a favor and mute the microphone!

- **Turn it off during a break.** Too many speakers have neglected to turn their microphone off at the break. As a result, the microphone often goes to the restroom with them! It's not a pretty sound, and I would highly suggest you not do that.

Headset microphones are also popular, and the newer ones are very slim and difficult for the audience to see, which is great. They come in different flesh tones so they blend in with your cheek. It's not really a headset anymore since the device slips over your ear like a Bluetooth device. The cord runs down the back of your neck and plugs into a receiver box that clips to your waist.

Some of the same guidelines apply to a headset as a lavaliere. One tip worth mentioning is to use a Band-Aid to tape the cord to the back of your neck in such a way that it creates a little slack at the ear so you do not feel a constant tug on the cord around your ear. Also, the Band-Aid pulls off a little easier than other types of tape.

Be Genuine, Humble, and Confident

I know that seems like a tall order, but it can be done. I have sat through all extremes, as many audience members have. I have watched speakers speak down to the audience and appear arrogant and cocky. You can be an expert on your topic and still remain humble. You can be confident in your material and delivery without being arrogant.

Being humble endears the audience to you. It lets them know you are not perfect. It allows the audience to connect with you. Talking down to an audience or talking over the heads of the audience will put a divide between you and the audience. The audience members want to know you are human just like they are.

I have heard experts on public speaking suggest that you lead the audience to believe that you are a genius by doing one thing or another. They actually suggest you mislead the audience through specific techniques that will cause the audience to think more highly of you. I would like to suggest otherwise. Always be genuine and truthful. Always be yourself. Trying to be something other than what you are will not endear an audience to you.

Creating a butt-kicking presentation requires a lot of time and focus on the delivery. Be patient and practice. Learn from your mistakes and the mistakes of others. Take input and suggestions from people you trust. Most importantly, never give up.

9

HOW TO GET THE FULL ATTENTION OF YOUR AUDIENCE

"What information consumes is rather obvious: it consumes the attention of its recipients. Hence a wealth of information creates a poverty of attention."
—*Herbert Simon*

I can't even begin to count the number of presentations I have sat through that have put me to sleep, nor can I begin to count the number of people I have watched fall asleep during presentations. The reason this happens is because so many speakers give half-brained presentations.

Many speakers simply provide facts and information which only engage one side of the brain. The other side of the brain is completely asleep. If a speaker wants to truly succeed in engaging the audience, they need to get the full attention of the audience and engage both sides of the brain.

Roger Sperry won the Nobel Prize in 1981 for research that can benefit every speaker and presenter. Sperry had conducted split brain surgery on epileptic patients to control their behavior. In the process, he discovered very specific functions of each side of the brain. Why is this pertinent to presenters? Because if presenters can understand what stimulates both sides of the brain, they can gain the *full* attention of their audience!

Roger Sperry was able to separate the communication of the left brain from the right brain. He then presented various visual and tactical information to the left and right side without the other side of the brain knowing it. The results were amazing.

While the patient had the communication cord severed in his brain (preventing the left and right sides from communicating with each other), he was still able to function normally. Well, almost. When presented with an object, like a pen, the right hand and eye could name the object but the patient was unable to explain what the pen was used for. When presented to the left hand and eye, the patient could demonstrate and explain the use of the object, but could not name it.

During the course of his research, Sperry discovered very distinctive functions of each side of the brain. Left brain functions include:

- Reasoning

- Math and science

- Comprehension

- Strategy

- Organizing

- Analyzing

- Logic

- Planning

- Detail processing

When a presenter stands up and throws out facts and information to the audience, the presenter is only engaging the left side of the brain. There is no need for the left side to communicate with the right side, because the functions of the right side are not required. The right side of the brain is completely asleep! This is why people get easily bored with presentations that overwhelm the audience with facts without adding any stimulus for the right brain. Functions of the right side of the brain include:

- Imagining

- Remembering

- Laughing

- Feeling

- Fantasy

- Risk-taking

- Sensing

Presenters will do themselves and the audience a huge favor by waking up the right side of the brain! When you have both sides of the brain involved in the presentation, you can keep people awake, interested, and involved. No one needs to work at stimulating left brain activity. Just standing up and presenting to people requires their left brain to "analyze" your information.

It's more of a challenge for some presenters to engage the right brain of their audience. Who do you think has the most trouble doing this? Left-brained individuals! People who are predominately left-brained in their thinking will tend to present in a left-brained manner. People who are right-brained thinkers tend to present in a right-brained format. Whether you are left-brained dominant or right-brained, you can still wake up the right side of the brains in your audience. There are specific things you can do or say that will stimulate right brain activity. Here are five practical tools to help you do that:

1) Storytelling

2) Props

3) Demonstrations

4) Activities

5) Humor

Storytelling

I have never met an audience that didn't appreciate a good story. Stories stimulate many of the functions of the right brain: imagining, fantasy, feeling, remembering, etc. There is nothing like a good story to wake up the right side of the brain.

Whenever you use the phrase "imagine this," or "picture this," you immediately stimulate right brain activity. When you begin to use word pictures to tell your story, the right brain comes to life! Obviously, if the story is boring and full of too much detail, your right brain will turn it over to the left brain and proceed to take a nap!

Stories that are touching or moving will tap into the "feeling" function of the right brain. Stories that are exciting, suspenseful, or far-fetched will tap into the "fantasy" function. Stories with a true moral to them will tap the "philosophy" function, and stories that are funny will tap the "humor" function. When using stories in your presentations, consider the following guidelines:

- **Keep the story relevant:** Don't just tell stories to wake up the right brain. Make sure the story applies to the topic and/or the audience. Make sure the audience can relate to the story. Also, make sure your story has a point. Otherwise, you'll just annoy the audience, which is a common function of the right *and* left brain!

- **Use Personal Stories:** You can always guarantee originality when you use your own stories. Dig around in your past for awhile and find some interesting, entertaining, funny, moving, or touching stories that you can incorporate into your presentations. These are also the easiest stories to remember.

- **Make your story vivid:** Any detail you provide should be for the purpose of getting the audience to actually picture your story. Get rid of any unnecessary detail that will just bore the audience or drag the story out too long.

- **Tweak your stories as needed:** You can alter your stories to appeal to specific audiences. You may add different details or segments that would be of more interest to architects than it would be to accountants. You can also design your story for a short length version and a long length version. This way, if you have much more time during a speaking engagement, you can expand the story.

- **Tell appropriate stories:** If you are ever in doubt as to whether your story is appropriate or not, don't tell it! If there is a chance you might offend anyone in the audience, don't tell it. All stories should be clean and in good taste.

- **Story Stretching:** I often introduce a story towards the beginning of my presentation. I will then incorporate many of the facts and statistics I may need to, and continue with the story later in the presentation. This keeps the suspense of the audience. I will often wait until the end of the presentation to finish the story or drop the bomb (the moral, the punch line, or the surprise twist).

- **Practice on Others:** Before you launch a story on your audience, try it out on someone else. Don't ask them what they think of your story until *after* you tell it. Just tell them the story in the normal course of your conversation and see if it gets a good laugh, or a tear if that's what you intended. Try it out on a small group of people. The response will let you know if the story will have the intended affect on other audiences.

Props

Props are a great way to stimulate right brain activity. Props can be humorous additions to your presentation, or merely a "visual" example of what you are talking about. Magic tricks or juggling items can be used as props in addition to many other things.

When I speak to audiences about communication and public speaking skills, I talk about this very issue of left brain and right brain activity. I actually take a good sized model of a brain as a prop. I hold it in my hand as I explain the different functions of each side of the brain. I say, "Imagine that this is the left side of your brain," and I proceed to provide the facts. While explaining the concept, the right brain is fully engaged as it visualizes exactly what I am saying.

I also use humorous pictures as props when I am giving presentations. I have some very funny photos that are blown up and embedded in my PowerPoint presentations. I also have some that are blown up and laminated so it's easy for the audience to see the pictures when I am not using PowerPoint. I usually get a good laugh out of the audience which wakes up the right brain. If you use props in your presentations, consider some of these guidelines:

- **Make the prop visible:** It's pretty annoying for people in the back of the room if they can't see the prop. If you have a very large audience and you don't have a way to magnify your prop, don't use it.

- **Make the prop relevant:** Don't just pull out funny things for people to look at or laugh at. I have seen presenters do this, and it really annoys people who want the presenter to get to the point. I have also seen many presenters really stretch the relevancy of their props. If you can't tie it into the presentation and really make it relevant, don't use it.

- **Consider portability:** If you have very large props and you have to fly to your presentation, you may want to reconsider your props. You want to make your travel as convenient as possible, and having to lug around huge props can be cumbersome. Think of creative ways to substitute large props for smaller ones. Brainstorm some ideas that would allow you to use a different prop and still have a strong impact in your presentation.

- **Passing props:** I have seen many presenters pass props around the room for people to look at. Sometimes the prop is a sample item of what the presenter is explaining. Keep in mind that when people get those props in their hands, they are no longer listening to what you are saying. In most cases, neither is the person on their right or left. In fact, they may even be talking to each other. Passing props can be very distracting to the speaker and the audience. I don't recommend passing props or items of demonstration to audience members. Instead, have the items available on a table to look at and try out during a break. This allows those who are actually interested to pick it up and inspect it.

Demonstrations

People tend to grasp your topic and presentation much more clearly when you provide demonstrations. A demonstration will engage the right side of the brain as the audience members attempt to assimilate the "big picture."

I often demonstrate some of the concepts I am trying to convey through the use of magic tricks. I'll give you an example: When I taught financial planning seminars at a community college, I spent a good deal of time educating the audience on taxes, inflation, and the need for diversification. Real exciting stuff, huh? It doesn't get more left-brained than that. Well, just about the time the right brain is ready to give up and go to sleep I say, "Let me give you a visual demonstration of what I am talking about."

People immediately sit up and appear more interested. The right brain has just come to life. I reach behind me and grab two foam cups from a table. One of the cups is nearly full of water and the other cup is empty. I pour the water from one cup into the other as I say, "Let's assume you pour all of your money into a savings account or a checking account and ignore diversification."

I finish pouring the water into the empty cup. I reach behind me again and pick up a pencil. I begin to poke it in the side of the cup as I say, "Taxes come along and poke a hole in your investments." I poke another hole into the other side of the cup. "Inflation comes along and pokes another hole in your investments."

Meanwhile, no water is coming out and the audience is dumbfounded. I poke one final hole in another part of the cup as I say, "And then a lack of diversification pokes another hole in your investments and before you know it, you have nothing left."

I turn the cup upside down and nothing comes out. The water appears to have completely evaporated into thin air! The audience is wide awake now and the right brain is completely engaged.

Demonstrations can also be used to show how an actual item works. If you are giving a presentation on a new network system for your company, there is nothing better than a demonstration to make your point.

If you have the time and opportunity to give a short demonstration, take it. Just be sure that you don't drag it out or bore your audience with how something works. Check the pulse of your audience and make sure they are interested in your demonstration.

If you incorporate demonstrations in your presentations, consider some of these guidelines:

- **Don't force people to participate in demonstrations:** If you need someone from the audience to help with the demonstration, ask for a volunteer. Never insist that someone participate in a demonstration.

- **Keep it short:** Long and drawn out demonstrations can bore your audience to tears. Keep the demonstration short and to the point.

- **Check regulations:** Check with the company, facility manager, or city to make sure your demonstration doesn't violate any regulations. I was asked to promote an event for a Rotary Club. The event was a "Sock Hop," and I was in charge of the public relations and advertising. At one of the Rotary meetings, I decided to ride in on a Harley to demonstrate my point. The local Harley shop brought down a huge bike for me from the show floor. It was clean and beautiful! They brought it on a trailer, and the bike had never touched pavement. The Rotary meeting was held in a city building, and much to my dismay, the manager of the facility showed up just as I was riding the motorcycle into the building. She nearly had a heart attack. Apparently, they don't allow that. There's a saying that really applied here: "It's easier to ask forgiveness than it is to ask permission." She was one very angry woman, and I had a lot of explaining to do.

- **Be familiar with the demonstration:** I attended a seminar once and the speaker decided to do a demonstration on a technologically advanced product that would help attendees with their time management. It turned out to be a comedy show when he couldn't figure out how to use the product and had to call his assistant up to show him how to work it. It was pretty embarrassing for the speaker, and cost him some credibility. Make sure you are familiar with any items you plan to demonstrate.

- **Be safe:** I once surveyed a large group of firefighters and I asked them what annoyed them most about some of the presenters and instructors they were subjected to. I had to laugh at some of the responses. A few of the surveys said, "Using explosives in class." Apparently, an instructor wanted to demonstrate one of the items he was teaching about and actually used the explosive in a demonstration... right in the classroom! Luckily, no one was hurt, but I can assure you, there were plenty of extremely irritated firefighters! Avoid demonstrating anything that has the potential to cause people harm.

Activities

Getting your audience involved in activities really keeps them engaged. It stimulates right and left brain activity, and heightens the learning process. People learn by observing, but they will learn even more by doing!

I once taught an eight-hour public speaking and communication skills class at an annual fire conference. Many of these firefighters had to get out and make presentations to community organizations and schools. I explained that keeping the attention of children can be a real challenge. I could have just given them some suggestions for speaking to kids: Tell stories, use props, make animal balloons (if you know how).

Instead, I involved the class in an activity. I brought hundreds of animal balloons and pumps, and I showed them how to make bumble-bee animal balloons. Everyone in the class participated in the activity. And I can assure you, there were no snoozers! The right brain was wide awake, and every classroom within a thirty foot radius could hear us twisting balloons! It was quite a sight, I must say. It also provides a tremendous amount of humor to the workshop, which also stimulates right brain activity.

I currently conduct keynotes as well as workshops on a variety of topics, including leadership. Some of these workshops last four, and sometimes eight hours. I incorporate a lot of activities and team-oriented exercises to keep the right brain engaged and the learning process heightened.

The all-time favorite in all of my workshops, regardless of the topic, is the remote control competition. All of my workshops that last three hours or more will include this activity. Depending on the size of the group, I give every two to six people a remote control to share as a "team." At different times in the workshop, we stop and take out our remotes. The program interfaces with my PowerPoint, so it is a smooth transition to what I call the "Electronic Competition."

There is a receiver unit at the front of the class that registers the answers of each remote. At the front of the room is a huge screen that displays the multiple choice questions. Questions are selected from various categories, similar to Jeopardy. The questions include information from the workshop as well as trivia pertinent to the industry of the particular audience.

As each team answers the questions, the program registers correct and incorrect answers and displays a running score for each team. As the workshop progresses, it becomes very exciting and competitive as everyone gets involved. It adds a tremendous amount of fun and right-brained activity to the seminar or workshop. The team with the most points by the end of the workshop wins prizes like books, CDs, or DVDs.

If you incorporate activities in your presentations, consider some of these guidelines:

- **Don't force people to participate in activities:** Always preface an activity by stating that it is optional. Usually, if you clearly define the purpose of the activity and the instructions, most people will participate.

- **Keep activities in teams:** Every activity I provide is done in groups of two or more. This takes the pressure off any one person to "perform," and adds camaraderie to the workshop. I have never had anyone refuse to do an activity in a group or team environment.

- **Keep it simple:** Don't overwhelm people with complicated activities that take a ten-page manual to figure out. Keep the activity simple and to the point.

- **Keep it short:** Don't assign long and drawn out activities. People will lose interest and will sometimes get up and leave the room because it's taking too long (I have to admit that I've left the room before in a situation like this). Activities are great for breaking up long presentations and workshops, but they should be kept to a bearable time limit.

- **Don't try to "squeeze" it in:** Shorter presentations should not include activities. If your workshop, seminar, or presentation is less than two hours in length, you probably don't have time for an in-depth activity. By the time you explain the activity and get everyone engaged, you have chewed up a good amount of time.

Humor

Have you ever been to a stand-up comedy routine? If so, have you ever noticed anyone dozing off, or sleeping? My bet is... No! Laughing is a major function of the right brain, and most people find it impossible to sleep while laughing. Everyone loves a speaker who can make them laugh while providing a valuable message. There are so many positive effects of humor, both for the audience and the speaker. This is such an important part of presenting, that I have committed an entire section of the book to this very topic. So, instead of repeating myself, I will let you read the next section.

10

USING HUMOR IN YOUR PRESENTATIONS

*"The wit makes fun of other persons;
the satirist makes fun of the world;
the humorist makes fun of himself."*
—James Thurber

Humor is an amazing thing. It alleviates stress and breaks down barriers. It is a physiological fact that stress and laughter cannot occupy the same space at the same time. As a speaker and presenter, I have had to face many stressed-out audiences! I have looked out into the faces of people who have had long weeks; people who had to come to my presentation because their boss forced them to; people who had stress building up at home; people who had high expectations of their presenters. As you can see, there can be a good amount of stress on both sides—stress from the audience and stress for the speakers as they attempt to break through that barrier.

Laughter is proven to be a great stress-buster. Everyone loves a funny speaker. But that doesn't mean you have to consider yourself a funny person to use humor in your presentations. There are lots of ways to incorporate humor without having to be a stand-up comedian. Some of the best sources of humor are right in front of you. Take a good look at your friends, family, and co-workers. Now there's something to laugh at! There are all kinds of stories and humorous situations that can be incorporated into your presentations. By far, the best source of humor is you. You can always poke fun at yourself and never risk offending the audience.

There are many sources of humor to draw from and add to your presentation. Some of them can be pre-planned, and some can be spontaneous. The sources for humor are endless. Here are some practical examples of what you can use:

Funny Videos

Whenever I give a presentation, I always take along my laptop computer which will interface with just about any LCD or DLP projector. I have collected over 400 short video clips that are hilarious. People send them to me via e-mail, and I come across some great ones on the web. I make sure the clips are appropriate to the audience, and I put together a PowerPoint show that cycles through the video clips. All of the videos have sound and I make sure the computer is hooked up to an adequate sound system or powerful speakers.

As the audience is coming in to sit down, they have something that grabs their attention immediately and puts them in a good mood. You can see the stressed-out faces begin to relax as the humor takes over. It sets a tone for lightheartedness and lets the audience know right off the bat that you have a sense of humor. Additionally, the audience isn't shifting impatiently in their seats, checking their watches as they are waiting for the presentation to start.

Funny Pictures

Whether you use PowerPoint, overheads, or slides, you can always throw in funny photos. Most of the time, the cartoons or photos relate directly to the topic at hand. However, there are times when I may have to cover a certain amount of dry material for training purposes. To lighten things up and keep the audience alert, I embed funny pictures and videos into my Power-Point presentation that are relevant to the topic.

I have taught a writing class in corporations and municipalities. Talk about a dry topic! "Now I would like to move on to the importance of proper grammar and punctuation when writing." ZZZZZZZZZZZZZZZZZZZZZZZZZZZZZZZZZZZZZZZZZ!

I incorporate a lot of humor and funny exercises to keep the class lively. In one section of the training, I talk about the importance of proofing your work. To visually depict my point, I put up a series of photos on the screen through my PowerPoint presentation. The photos include signs with missing letters and misspelled words that create a completely different meaning. This always gets a good laugh.

One example is a huge sign over a fast food restaurant that was missing a vital letter. The sign reads: "Now hiring losers" instead of "Now hiring closers." I have lots of photos that add plenty of humor to the presentation.

Printed Mistakes Get Good Laughs

These are not too difficult to find. You can search the web for these and you'll end up with more than you know what to do with. Church bulletins are always a big hit in my presentations. I use these in training for writing and communication skills. I lead into the church bulletins by saying something like, "Communication skills are imperative. What we intend to communicate is not always what is received. Let me share some examples with you from some actual church bulletins."

I proceed to either bring them up on the screen in Power-Point or read them from a list. The audience loves them and it always produces a good laugh. Some examples of the ones I have used are:

- Pastor is on vacation. Massages can be given to church secretary.

- The rosebud on the alter this morning is to announce the birth of David Alan Belzer, the sin of Rev. and Mrs. Julius Belzer.

- The Weight Watchers Group will meet Thursdays at 7:00 PM. Please use double doors at side entrance.

- The Associate Minister unveiled the church's new tithing campaign slogan last Sunday: "I Upped My Pledge – Up Yours!"

- Ladies, don't forget the rummage sale on Saturday. It's a chance to get rid of all the useless things around the house. Bring your husbands.

- The church will be sponsoring a "New Mother's Group." All those wishing to become "New Mothers," please see the pastor in his study.

Funny headlines are also a great source of humor for presentations. It's not too difficult to find some to fit your topic. Additionally, you can tie in the concept of miscommunication in just about any presentation. A quick Internet search will produce a long list of funny headlines that can be used to fit your presentation. Here are some examples of funny headlines (you actually have to stop and think about a few of these):

- Police Begin Campaign to Run Down Jaywalkers

- Safety Experts Say School Bus Passengers Should Be Belted

- Panda Mating Fails; Veterinarian Takes Over

- Plane Too Close to Ground, Crash Probe Told

- Miners Refuse to Work after Death

- Juvenile Court to Try Shooting Defendant

- Two Sisters Reunited after 18 Years in Checkout Counter

- Never Withhold Herpes Infection from Loved One

- If Strike isn't Settled Quickly, It May Last a While

- Typhoon Rips Through Cemetery; Hundreds Dead

- New Study of Obesity Looks for Larger Test Group

I have also found a lot of misprinted advertising, road signs, and business signs that provide a good source of humor in my training. I would highly suggest that you constantly update much of the humor you use so your audiences do not come to expect the same old thing. When this happens, the humor loses the intended effect.

Short Jokes
I suggest short jokes, because not only are longer jokes harder to remember and tell, they require a much higher level of humor. The longer it takes to get to the punch line, the funnier the joke or story has to be. Short jokes can be modified to seem

more like true stories that surprise the audience with a punch line. For example, I speak on communication skills quite a bit. I use a short joke that I convert to appear as a true story:

> "In communication, one of the key elements is listening. This is not always easy if you have someone who doesn't listen. I was talking to my uncle last week, and he was telling me about his recent doctor's appointment. He told his doctor that he didn't think my aunt's hearing was as good as it used to be and wondered what he should do.
>
> The doctor told him, 'Why don't you try this test to find out for sure. When your wife is in the kitchen doing dishes or cooking, stand about fifteen feet behind her and ask her a question. If she doesn't respond, keep moving closer and ask the question again—keep asking it until she hears you.'
>
> So my uncle went home to find my aunt fixing dinner. He stood fifteen feet behind her and asked, 'What's for dinner, honey?' No response. He moved to about ten feet behind her and asked again, 'Honey, what's for dinner?' Still no response. He moved within five feet—still no answer.
>
> Finally, he stood directly behind her and asked loudly, 'Honey, what's for dinner?'
>
> My aunt spun around with a frustrated and disgusted look on her face and yelled, 'For the *fourth time*, I said *chicken!*'
>
> We often think it's the other person who has a hard time listening, when it might be us."

This creates an unexpected end and the audience can relate to this humor. Everyone has to deal with listening and communication problems.

Short jokes and stories should always be tied into the topic matter and be relevant. I never tell a joke just for the sake of making the audience laugh. The humor needs to have a point.

One of the topics I speak on is overcoming adversity. I have a tremendous amount of experience in that area, and the adversity I have endured throughout my life can often leave a heavy tone with the audience. It's perfectly acceptable to take the audience to that depth, but sometimes it's necessary to provide them with an outlet and a sense of relief from a painful topic. Humor is a good way to accomplish this. When I talk about adversity, I might throw in a short joke that I have turned into a story to provide a change of pace. Here's an example:

"No one is immune to adversity. A photographer for a national magazine was assigned to get photos of a huge forest fire. The smoke at the scene was too thick to get any quality photos, so he frantically called his home office and asked for a plane. His editor assured him it would be taken care of. Sure enough, when the photographer arrived at the small, rural airport, there was a little plane warming up near the runway. The photographer jumped in with his equipment and yelled, 'Let's go! Let's go!'

The pilot quickly swung the plane into the wind and off they went. 'Fly over the north side of the fire,' the photographer yelled, 'and make three or four low level passes.'

'Why?' the pilot asked.

'So I can get the pictures! I'm the photographer, and the photographer gets the pictures!' He was in a hurry to get the scene of the fire and was getting pretty annoyed at this point.

After a very long pause the pilot looked over at him and said, 'So, *you're* not the instructor?'"

This produces huge laughs. It's a very unexpected twist, and it comes at a great time in the presentation. It gives the audience relief and shifts the tone of the presentation. It's perfectly acceptable to intertwine humor and seriousness in the same presentation. However, it does need to be strategically placed and not used in a haphazard manner.

Proverbs, Sayings, and One-Liners

Many speakers do not take advantage of the many one-liners out there that can be used. Even some of the older ones can be changed and modernized. Also, many one-liners or clichés can be re-written for an even more humorous effect. They can also be adapted to relate to the specific event or the audience.

A great source for one-liners is the web. There are lots of funny proverbs, sayings, and one-liners. Be creative and change them to suit your topic or audience. Intertwine them in your stories and use them to lighten the mood.

Taking old sayings and proverbs and changing them is always a fun way to lighten up the audience. Also, taking old Confucius sayings and making them funny gets a good laugh. There are lots of sayings, proverbs, and one-liners that work great. Here are some examples:

- He who laughs last… has found someone to blame.

- A penny saved… is not worth bending over to pick up anymore.

- Confucius says: Man who run in front of car get tired; man who run behind car get exhausted.

114

- Confucius says: Man who stands on toilet, high on pot.

- It takes a big man to cry. It takes an even bigger man to laugh at that man.

- Some days you're the dog; some days you're the fire hydrant.

- If at first you don't succeed... destroy all evidence that you ever tried.

- It used to be only death and taxes were inevitable. Now, of course, there's shipping and handling, too.

- That which doesn't kill you... will make you wish you were dead!

- Give a man a fish, feed him for a day; teach a man to fish and he'll sit in a boat all day and drink beer.

- The things that come to those that wait may be the things left by those who got there first.

- A pessimist is someone who finally sees the handwriting on the wall and then claims it's a forgery.

- It's all right to sit on your pity pot every now and again. Just be sure to flush when you are done.

- There are two kinds of people in the world: The people who like their jobs and the people who don't work here anymore.

- I started out with nothing and I still have most of it.

Stupid or Funny Quotes by Famous People

People love to hear funny or stupid things that were said by someone else. They especially love it when they know the person. Famous quotes are always a big hit, especially when you tie them in with your topic. Below are just a few examples.

(These were sent to me via email and can be found on the web):

- Steve Martin: "A day without sunshine is like, you know, night."

- George Bush, US President: "I have opinions of my own—strong opinions—but I don't always agree with them."

- Matt Lauer: "Researchers have discovered that chocolate produces some of the same reactions in the brain as marijuana.... The researchers also discovered other similarities between the two, but can't remember what they are."

- Brooke Shields: "Smoking kills people and if you're killed, you've lost a very important part of your life."

- Mayor Marion Barry, Washington DC: "Outside of the killings, Washington has one of the lowest crime rates in the country."

- Mariah Carey: "Whenever I watch TV and see those poor starving kids all over the world, I can't help but cry. I mean I'd love to be skinny like that but not with all those flies and death and stuff."

- Miss Alabama in the 1994 Miss USA contest was asked this question: "If you could live forever, would you and why?" Her answer: "I would not live forever, because we should not live forever, because if we were supposed to live forever, then we would live forever, but we cannot live forever, which is why I would not live forever."

- A congressional candidate in Texas: "That lowdown scoundrel deserves to be kicked to death by a jackass, and I'm just the one to do it."

- Dick Clark: "Humor is always based on a modicum of truth. Have you ever heard a joke about a father-in-law?"

- Aristotle: "Mothers are fonder than fathers of their children because they are more certain they are their own."

Using the Audience for Humor

When you create a humorous environment in your presentations, the audience will normally pick up on it and provide you with many sources of humor. In a seminar setting where you encourage participation, this is especially true.

I was teaching a financial planning seminar many years ago. I had a gentleman sitting right in the front who was 82 years old and had a completely bald head. His name was Selwyn. He was very funny and was always adding comments here and there that made everyone laugh.

During the second hour of the seminar, I was talking about inflation. I gave examples of prices on goods and services thirty years ago versus today. I asked the audience to tell me how much they were paying for a loaf of bread. I then asked how much they were paying for a dozen of eggs. I finally asked how much a man's haircut was going for. Just as the words left my lips, I made eye contact with Selwyn. Without missing a beat he replied dryly, "I have no idea." He began rubbing the top of his bald head. The room burst out in laughter. It was perfect timing.

Your audience is a great source of laughter when you let them bring out some of the humor. In many seminars, there is camaraderie between the people present who know each other. They will often make jokes or create a humorous atmosphere if the speaker facilitates this and sets the tone.

Audience humor is also the most natural and spontaneous form of humor. The best way to tap into this form of humor is to facilitate a participatory environment. Encourage questions, discussion, and activities. As you do, humorous personalities will emerge with quick wit and humorous anecdotes.

The key to allowing the audience to provide a good deal of humor in your presentations is keeping control. As a speaker, you have to know when to rein people in and move the topic along. Timing is important, and appropriate humor is imperative.

Speakers should never single people out in an audience and use them as a source of humor. This can be very embarrassing and uncomfortable for some people, and I do not recommend it. The only exception would be asking for a volunteer for a demonstration or magic trick that is humorous. In these cases, the audience member usually knows they will be made fun of, and they choose to take that chance. Those who volunteer can usually take the heat. As I pointed out earlier, you just don't want to force people to participate.

Industry-Specific Humor

I always find some form of humor that is specific to my audience. If I am talking to architects, I will find a good joke or one-liner. If I am talking to firefighters, I do the same. I can always come up with a story or joke that applies to the audiences and makes them laugh. It doesn't matter who the audience is— there is humor to be found.

The best way to find industry-specific humor is through a web search. When I speak to people in the medical industry, I do a web search for "medical jokes and humor." If I'm speaking to police officers, I search under "police jokes and humor." It's really simple, and you will always find something.

What to Expect with Humor

I have discovered a very important fact about humor. Not all humor lands the same on all audiences. I have used a one-liner or short joke on one audience and they just howled. I have used the exact same humor on another audience and received little to no response. A few factors that determine how humor will be received:

- **The Time of Day:** Early morning audiences do not like to laugh all that much. It's almost impossible to get belly laughs out of people in the morning. Why do you think all stand-up comedy routines are held in the evening? If everyone was in a laughing mood in the morning, comedians wouldn't be performing at night. Unfortunately, there's the flip side to that: most people are more attentive in the morning. If you want them to be attentive in the afternoon or evening, you need to get them laughing (or engage their right brain in some other creative way). When you end up as the last speaker of a conference or you end up speaking at the end of the day, people are tired and don't have a lot of energy to offer. If they have been sitting through presentations all day, you'll have much more of a challenge getting them to laugh in the afternoon or evening, but it can be done! "Humor is by far the most significant activity of the human brain." —Edward De Bono

- **Audience Mix:** A mix of male and female audience members provides great laughter. I have given the exact same presentation to an all-male audience as I have to a mixed audience, and the difference is very noticeable. Men tend to lighten up more when there are more women around laughing. Otherwise, they don't reveal too much emotion around an all-male audience. Maybe they think other guys won't think they're macho enough. Or maybe they want to see if other guys are going to laugh too. I have found all-female audiences to be the best receptors of humor. They are free to laugh and are much quicker to lighten up.

- **Audience Culture:** If I am speaking to a corporate audience and there has been turmoil in the organization, it's more of a challenge to get them to laugh. I have to hit on some issues that they can all relate to, and help them to find the humor in some of the difficulties. I do a lot of training in fire departments. I have found that if the upper management is present in some of the training, the attendees are not as likely to let go with the laughter unless the upper management does. The tone is usually set by the "chiefs," and attendees will normally follow their lead.

A Few Simple Rules

While humor is widely accepted and greatly needed in presentations, there are still some guidelines you should follow. If you keep a few simple rules in mind, you can avoid potential humor disasters. You want all of your humor to be well-received and remembered in a positive light.

- **Keep it clean:** You should never use inappropriate or off-color humor. If in doubt, throw it out!

- **Know your audience:** Some things won't be as funny to certain groups. Know who you are speaking to and make sure they don't have any "sore spots" that might be touchy.

- **Try it on someone else first:** If you're not sure how your joke or humor will be received, try it out on someone other than your audience. Find people who will honestly tell you if it's funny or not.

- **Keep it relevant:** Make sure your humor has a point, especially in business settings. While people love to be entertained, they also consider their learning and training time valuable. Make sure the humor is relevant to the topic and has a point. Humor should be used to reinforce your message and lighten things up.

- **Singing Humor:** If you ever plan to sing in a presentation, you had better be one of two things (or both):

   1) Very good
   2) Very funny

   I have seen far too many speakers attempt to throw in a singing routine somewhere in the presentation, and it's just plain painful for the audience. You don't have to be able to sing if it's funny, especially if you acknowledge you can't sing. If you plan to attempt a serious singing routine in a presentation, you had better know how to sing!

- **Don't belittle audience members for a laugh:** Sometimes it seems irresistible to pick on someone in the audience to make everyone laugh. Don't do it. You will end up isolating members of your audience and embarrassing others. It's just not worth it. Pick on yourself—there's plenty of material there, I can assure you.

Humor Resources

There are so many sources of humor—you just have to look around. You can observe funny things in other people. You can watch your family. You can read funny newsletters and books. You can rent stand-up comedy videos. You can go to a comedy club and see how it's done. There is a wide variety of humorous speakers that you can listen to in person or on tape. You can access the Internet and find more humor than you know what to do with. Search for things like:

- Funny web sites

- Web sites with funny quotes

- Web sites with funny videos

- Daily humor sites

- Funny cartoon sites

- Good clean humor sites

Humor is such a powerful tool in presenting. I can't reiterate enough how important self-effacing humor is. There is plenty of material when we examine ourselves. I don't have to look very far to find my faults, idiosyncrasies, failures, and other humorous items I can use. Each and every one of us has a plethora of funny stories we can draw from. The more original the material, the better it is received. Using stories from your own life and the people in your family is a great way to use humor.

Additionally, you stand a pretty high chance that the audience has not heard the humor if you are sharing personal stories (of course that also depends on how big of a mouth your friends and family members may have!). Use humor with class.

"Humor is the great thing, the saving thing. The minute it crops up, all our irritations and resentments slip away and a sunny spirit takes their place."
—Mark Twain

11

USING VISUAL AIDS

"While modern technology has given people powerful new communication tools, it apparently can do nothing to alter the fact that many people have nothing useful to say."
—Leo Gomes

I walked in the conference center with great expectations. There were numerous sessions to select from. Most of the workshops ranged from forty-five minutes to an hour. I selected my first one and found my seat.

The speaker began the session with a brief introduction and immediately turned to the big projection screen behind him. Because he didn't have a microphone on, when he turned his back to the audience, we could barely hear his voice.

He proceeded to click his remote mouse as he navigated through his PowerPoint presentation. He never turned around and looked at us again. He simply read each line on every slide and then progressed to the next slide. After about fifteen minutes, people began to get up and leave. He never even noticed! He just kept reading his PowerPoint slides with his back to the audience. He gave his entire presentation to the screen.

Unfortunately, many of the presentations at the conference were similar. If the speaker wasn't talking to the screen, they were fumbling with overhead transparencies. Most of the presenters using PowerPoint were not using it in a manner that enhanced their presentations. Most of the speakers used their visual aids to replace them as the presenter, and the audience was completely bored as a result.

Visual aids are intended to compliment a presentation, not replace the speaker. That is why they are called "aids." Far too many speakers neglect to develop their public speaking skills as they hide behind a slide projector, an overhead projector, or a PowerPoint presentation.

Visual aids can improve learning up to 400%! People are willing to pay nearly 30% more for a product or service when visual aids are used in the presentation. Incorporating visual aids into your presentation will add impact and your audience will retain more of what you said. However, if visual aids are not used correctly, you can bore your audience to death! Below are some common visual aids and some general tips when using them.

PowerPoint Presentations: The most popular visual aid today seems to be PowerPoint. It can be an excellent tool to enhance your presentation, but far too many presenters depend on PowerPoint too heavily and use it incorrectly. I have seen many speakers try to replace themselves with PowerPoint. *You* are the presentation, not your visual aids. If you plan to use PowerPoint, consider these guidelines:

- *Know how to use your equipment!* I have endured many presentations where the speaker was unfamiliar with the laptop computer or the projector. I watched one speaker fumble around trying to figure out how to launch his

PowerPoint presentation. He didn't even know how to bring it up on the computer screen. After watching the audience fidget and squirm, I finally offered to run the equipment for him. When speakers don't know how to use the equipment, it distracts from the presentation, annoys the audience, and hurts the speaker's credibility. If you are a presenter and you can't even use your own equipment, you shouldn't be allowed to play with anything sharper than a bowling ball.

- ***Have a back up plan:*** I was giving a presentation at a beautiful restaurant near the ocean one winter. There was a nasty storm, but my presentation was still scheduled. I arrived early and set everything up, and ten minutes into the presentation, the electricity went out. I had to conduct the rest of the presentation without PowerPoint. Luckily, I had other props and visual aids that I could use to make many of my points. You should always have a back up plan in case your equipment fails or something goes wrong. I have had my computer lock up, the projector fail, the electricity go out, etc. I always try to remain flexible and adapt as necessary. "Blessed are the flexible, for they shall not be broken." *—Unknown*

- ***Set up early:*** It's always best to set up at least thirty minutes before your presentation so you have time to troubleshoot your equipment. If I am using someone else's projector with my laptop, I will give myself forty-five minutes to set up and test everything. I have had to use that time on many occasions to work out bugs and problems. It's much better to have extra time available before your presentation than to be stressed and rushed to get everything up and working.

- ***Keep fonts large:*** The minimum font size you should be using is 24 pt. Audience members hate sitting through PowerPoint presentations where they have to squint to see the text. Presenters attempt to squeeze too much information on one slide. Fonts should be large enough to read.

- *Use points, not paragraphs:* PowerPoint should be used to make points and display concepts. Paragraphs of information should be avoided, as it bores your audience, is difficult to read, and looks terrible. Four to eight bulleted points per slide combined with some quality graphics will help make your point. Also, bring up each point as you address it so the audience is not reading ahead while you are trying to talk. You can set this up in the slide transition section of PowerPoint.

- *Don't overuse clipart:* Try to find new and updated graphics and clipart. Audiences get very tired of seeing the same pictures and graphics over and over. I use my digital camera and take a lot of my own pictures for my graphics so I know they're always original. I also utilize other online resources for graphics instead of just using clipart.

- *Lose all the fluff:* I once saw a presentation done by a police officer. The first line of text came in to the sound of a machine gun. Everyone laughed. It was pretty cute. Little did we know that he planned to bring in *every* line of text with that same sound. By the fifth line, we were very annoyed. By the twentieth line, we were ready to turn the machine gun on ourselves! It was awful. Limit any sounds or special effects when using PowerPoint. Too much fluff overloads the audience and becomes a distraction.

- *Be consistent in your presentation:* I sat through a PowerPoint presentation at a conference that drove me crazy. Every line of text had a different transition. Each slide had a different background. Slide headings had different fonts on every slide. Different font colors were used on each slide. Enough already! Maybe the presenter thought this would keep the audience awake. That is not the job of PowerPoint; that is the job of the presenter. Pick a template and go with it. Keep your fonts, colors, and backgrounds consistent. Otherwise, you will annoy and distract your audience, and that's bad.

- *Use light backgrounds:* Light colored backgrounds usually work best. I often use a white and light blue background that works wonderfully. It projects brightly and is easy to see. Darker backgrounds require a dim room or a very powerful projection unit. Darker backgrounds are also harder to see.

- *Use compatible font colors:* Different font colors are more difficult to see with certain backgrounds. It's best to find the most contrasting colors possible. Also, avoid using yellow and other light colors that strain the eyes from the back of the room.

- *Avoid fancy fonts:* Stick with your basic font styles for legibility. Titles and headlines can have a little more flare to them, but the standard font throughout the presentation should be an easy-to-read font. Times New Roman or Arial are best.

- *Don't talk to the screen:* Many presenters make this mistake. When using PowerPoint, they turn to the screen to read the text as they turn their back on the audience. I always put my laptop somewhere in front of me so I can always see what is being projected behind me. I never turn my back on the audience. Audiences want you to connect with them, and they want to know you are real. You really can't accomplish that when you're reading to a screen. Present to your audience, not the screen.

- *Use a black screen when you're telling stories or not using PowerPoint:* I always insert black slides in my PowerPoint presentations in the sections where I know I am going to tell stories, use props, or take questions. If you leave PowerPoint up on the screen, it will draw the attention of the audience to the screen instead of you. The audience also has a mental anticipation of the next slide if you leave the PowerPoint slide up there without a black screen. To get the full attention of your audience, darken that screen. Another way to make the screen go black is to walk over to your keyboard and hit the "B" key on the keyboard. This will cause the PowerPoint screen to turn black. To remove the black screen and continue your PowerPoint presentation, simply click your remote mouse or hit "Enter" on your keyboard.

- *Stay clear of the line of projection:* When using Power-Point, you need to stay clear of the projection light. When you walk in front of it, it blinds you for a second and casts a distracting shadow on the screen. It's best to have the projection over the heads of the audience so this is not an issue. This way, you can move freely around the room. Projectors that are mounted from a ceiling are usually the best. Otherwise, projectors often limit the speaker to standing on one side of the room. If I am stuck with a lower projection line, I will spend some time on one side of the room and then move to the other side of the room and spend some time over there.

- *Use quality equipment:* Whether using an LCD or DLP with your laptop, use quality equipment. Low lumens means you will have to dim the lights or even turn them off. You want to keep the room as lit as possible, and to accomplish that, you need projectors with high lumens (I prefer 3,000 and above). Low-lit rooms result in bored and sleepy audiences. Also, make sure your laptop computer and software is up-to-date as well. Attempting to use old technology with a laptop will slow down your graphics and the efficiency of PowerPoint. Sophisticated business audiences expect modern technology and quality equipment. More importantly, they want you to have something valuable to say, so don't rely so heavily on your PowerPoint.

Overhead Transparencies: Some presenters still use overhead projectors and transparencies (hard to believe, I know). The advantage to this type of visual aid is flexibility in textual content. Speakers can actually write on the overheads or fill in information for the audience. They can have blank transparencies on hand to add information as needed. When I taught financial planning classes at a local college, I used overhead transparencies for a period of four years. The overhead transparencies coincided perfectly with the pages in the workbooks, so attendees could follow along very easily. The information that needed to be filled in on the workbook also needed to be filled in on the overheads. It was simple, clear, and concise. There are drawbacks to using overhead transparencies (like portability), and the following factors and guidelines should be considered:

- *Handwriting needs to be legible:* If you write on overhead transparencies, people need to be able to read it. Sloppy handwriting is extremely irritating to the audience, especially if they can't read it.

- *Overheads need to be legible:* Too many presenters give overhead projector presentations with illegible and unprofessional overhead transparencies. The text is often too small to read, or the quality of the overhead is very poor. Text size should be large and a limited amount of information should be included on each overhead.

- *Use pen colors that are easy to see:* Black is always safe. Dark blue also works well. Avoid using yellow as it is too light and difficult to see.

- *Check overhead after placing it on the projector:* There are times when the speaker places an overhead on the projector and then continues to talk. The presenter doesn't bother to glance back at the screen to see if it's centered, focused, or upside down! I have watched a speaker go on and on until someone finally pointed out that the overhead was upside down and out of focus. A quick glance over the shoulder will alleviate this problem. Make sure the overheads are focused and straight. Otherwise, they become a distraction instead of a visual aid.

- *Don't stand in the line of projection:* It's very frustrating for an audience when a speaker is writing on an overhead and their shoulder is blocking half of the projection. You can look out at the audience and see everyone leaning to the side in an attempt to see the text. It takes a little practice, but you can learn to write on overheads from the side and not block the projection. Try it.

- *Turn off the projector when not referencing your overhead:* When a speaker uses a lot of overhead transparencies, the audience comes to expect them throughout the presentation. If you are done making a point with an overhead, and you start to talk about something else, the audience will still be glancing at the screen in anticipation of the next overhead unless you turn off the projector. If you turn the projector off, this tells the audience that you want their full attention on your words and not the screen. It also signals that you will not be tossing another overhead up there right away, so the audience will stop anticipating that. If you leave the projector on while talking about something other than what is on the screen, it becomes a distraction.

- ***Have a backup bulb handy.*** When I used an overhead projector (many, many, many years ago), I always had at least one extra projection bulb with me in case the lamp burned out. I have seen presenters lose a lamp in the middle of a presentation and then fumble for a backup due to lack of preparation. Don't do that.

Flip Charts: Presenters often use flip charts as a visual aid to help depict their point. Flip charts are also great for writing down audience feedback to specific questions. I have also used flip charts to keep track of team scores when I have competitive activities in workshops. If you plan to use flipcharts, consider the following guidelines and considerations:

- ***Write legibly:*** The audience needs to be able to read your handwriting. If you have atrocious handwriting like me, ask someone in the audience to come up and write down the points. You can also have some of your visual aids on your flip charts done ahead of time by someone who writes neatly.

- ***Make sure everyone can see the chart:*** Flip charts are not effective with very large audiences. People towards the back of the room cannot see the flip charts. Even with small audiences, you need to write large and clearly, and make sure that every person in the room can see the flip chart.

Videos: Training workshops often incorporate videos. There are many quality videos out there that can enhance a training topic or support a point. If you plan to use any videos in your presentation, consider the following guidelines:

- ***Don't use videos as a babysitter:*** Many presenters who use videos in training often turn down the lights, pop the tape in, and then leave the room for thirty minutes while everyone slowly nods off. You should never leave the room during a presentation unless it's a legitimate break.

- ***Keep it brief:*** If you show videos, do it in brief segments of five minutes or less. Pause the video and make comments or facilitate discussion. Your audience will tire quickly if the video goes on and on and on...

- ***Try to keep the lights up:*** Most videos can be shown in a fully lit room. Whenever you can avoid turning down the lights, take advantage of it. Dimly lit rooms lull audiences to sleep, especially if they have to watch a dull video. So if it's at all possible, make the video interesting and keep the room lit.

- ***Don't use outdated videos:*** Presenters who use outdated information in any form will lose credibility with the audience. I sat through a presentation last year that included some video instruction and information. All of the people in the video had hairstyles from the 70's and clothes from that same era. Everything was completely outdated and corny. It was difficult to take the information seriously, knowing how outdated it was.

General Visual Aid Guidelines

Visual aids can be a positive enhancement to your presentations if used properly. Otherwise, they can be a distraction and even a detriment if used incorrectly. Regardless of the visual aid you choose to use, there are some general guidelines that should be followed:

- ***Become familiar with the room in advance:*** Make sure every person in the room will be able to see your visual aid. Determine where you will be standing when you are speaking and where your visual aids will be located. Make sure there are no "blind spots" in the room where certain members of the audience will be unable to see clearly.

- *Check for typos and misspellings:* I have learned the hard way that I need to have someone else proof my PowerPoint slides. I don't always catch my own errors. Any visual aids that are used in a presentation need to be thoroughly proofed for accuracy and professionalism.

- *Check for appropriateness:* Make sure your visual aids are appropriate and politically correct. If you are in doubt as to whether your visual aids might offend someone, don't use them.

- *Use high quality visual aids*: Regardless of what type of visual aid you use, make sure the quality reflects your professionalism. The visual aids you choose will be a direct reflection on you as the presenter.

- *Provide handouts:* If you really want people to remember the information you presented in your PowerPoint presentation, slide show, overheads, or videos, provide handouts to take home. Handouts should always be clear, crisp, and high quality. I have received handouts that were outdated, photocopied from copies, crooked, and difficult to read. Again, this is a direct, negative reflection on the presenter. Unprofessional materials make for an unprofessional presentation. Don't let it happen to you. Also, you can save paper and provide handouts in a PDF format online where people can download them, which is what I do.

- **Room lighting:** Check out the room lighting in advance. I use PowerPoint a lot, and it's a much better presentation if there are not lights shining directly on the projection screen. Some rooms allow you to adjust certain segments of lights separately. This allows you to turn the lights down in the front of the room where the screen is and still keep the rest of the room fully lit. Some rooms do not have this option. I have actually asked for a ladder and I have unscrewed the lights just over the screen for a better presentation. Don't be afraid to have the room adjusted to enhance your visual aids as much as possible.

- *Laser pointers:* If you use a laser pointer with your visual aids, do everyone a favor and *hold it still*! It's very aggravating to have a presenter who waves that laser pointer all over the screen and constantly has it jumping up and down. Point to the area of interest and hold it there. Also, don't wave the laser pointer out at the audience—you could put someone's eye out with that thing! If you don't know how to use a laser pointer properly, you shouldn't be allowed out in public unsupervised.

Visual aids can be a great enhancement to your presentation or an unfortunate distraction. Visual aids will never make you a great presenter or public speaker. Just remember that the audience is looking to *you* for a great presentation, so the best visual aid you can possibly use is your body language of sincerity, enthusiasm, and passion for your topic. Be the best speaker you can be and your visual aids will serve their intended purpose: to aid you in enhancing audience attention and retention of your topic.

12

THE FOUR TYPES OF
SPEAKERS IN THE WORLD

*"Make happy those who are near,
and those who are far will come."*
—*Chinese Proverb*

While there are many different styles of speakers, there
are still four basic kinds of speakers in the world. This chapter
will examine each type of speaker as well as the potential
strengths and weaknesses each will possess.

Many speakers present to audiences based on their own social style and what they would prefer. As Herb Cohen put it,
"You and I do not see things as they are; we see things as *we*
are." Our paradigm is based on our own likes, preferences, and
styles.

Very technical and analytical people tend to favor numbers,
details, charts, and graphs. If they are asked to give a presentation, they tend to present in a manner that appeals to their own

preferences and styles instead of taking into consideration the preferences of the audience. As a result, many of the audience members become bored or annoyed.

There are four basic types of speakers, and four kinds of people in every audience. These four types of people consist of the four basic social styles. The information in this chapter and the next is derived from another book I have co-authored with Bob Phillips, Ph.D. (*How to Deal with Annoying People*).

In this section I would like to take you through the simple process of recognizing the four types of speakers and what some of their basic characteristics are. In the next section, we will look at the four kinds of people in the audience, and how to appeal to each social style in a presentation so everyone is taken into consideration.

Finding Your Own Social and Speaking Style

The first step is finding out what your own social style is, and what your tendencies will be as a speaker. Then you can examine the other social styles and what their expectations are as audience members, and how to adapt to meet their needs (next chapter).

There are four basic social styles: Analytical, Driver, Amiable, and Expressive. Your particular style will determine the basic manner in which you make a presentation. By identifying your style, you can work on your areas of weakness and highlight your areas of strength.

Let's begin by determining if you are an asker or a teller. There are two lists in Chart 12-A describing the characteristics of an asker and a teller. Which list describes you more—asker or teller? You may find that there are some characteristics in both lists that describe you, but one will usually describe you more than the other. Select either *ask* or *tell*.

Chart 12-A

ASK CHARACTERISTICS	TELL CHARACTERISTICS
☐ Less assertive, more introverted	☐ More assertive, more extroverted
☐ Outward response under stress: flight	☐ Outward response under stress: fight
☐ Driving emotion and motivation under stress: fear	☐ Driving emotion and motivation under stress: anger
☐ Communicates hesitantly	☐ Readily communicative
☐ Lower quantity of talk	☐ Higher quantity of talk
☐ Pace of speech: slower	☐ Pace of speech: faster
☐ Speech volume: softer	☐ Speech volume: louder
☐ Body movements: slow and deliberate	☐ Body movements: fast and rapid
☐ More tentative and less forceful	☐ Less tentative and more forceful
☐ Reserves opinions	☐ Shares opinions easily
☐ Less confrontive	☐ More confrontive
☐ Nonaggressive	☐ More aggressive
☐ Thoughtful decisions	☐ More decisive
☐ Will not pressure other for decisions	☐ Will pressure others for decisions
☐ Patient	☐ Impatient
☐ Not a huge risk taker	☐ More of a risk taker
☐ Avoids the use of power if at all possible	☐ Will use personal and positional power
☐ Attentive listener	☐ Has difficulty listening

Merrill and Reid, *Personal Styles and Effective Performance*; Robert Bolton and Dorothy G. Bolton, *Social Style/Management Style* (New York, NY: AMACOM, 1984) adapted.

☐   I see myself as more *asking*
☐   I see myself as more *telling*

The next step is to determine if you are task-oriented or relationship-oriented. Check the appropriate boxes on the next page.

Chart 12-B

TASK CHARACTERISTICS	RELATIONSHIP CHARACTERISTICS
☐ Dress: more formal ☐ Topics of speech: current issues and tasks at hand ☐ Body posture: more rigid ☐ Facial expressions: more controlled ☐ General attitude: more towards the serious side ☐ More reserved ☐ Controlled and guarded emotions ☐ Filled with facts and data ☐ Less interested in small talk ☐ Decisions are fact-based ☐ Disciplined about time ☐ Strict and disciplined about rules ☐ Restrained and guarded when sharing opinions ☐ Hard to get to know, keeps distance from others ☐ Preoccupied	☐ Dress: more informal ☐ Topics of speech: people, stories and anecdotes ☐ Body posture: more relaxed ☐ Facial expressions: more animated ☐ General attitude: more towards the playful side ☐ More outgoing ☐ Free to share emotions ☐ Filled with opinions and stories ☐ More interested in small talk ☐ Decisions are feeling or "gut-based" ☐ Less disciplined about time ☐ More permissive and lenient about rules ☐ More impulsive and forceful when sharing opinions ☐ Easy to get to know, does not keep distance from others ☐ More carefree

Merrill and Reid, *Personal Styles and Effective Performance*; Robert Bolton and Dorothy G. Bolton, *Social Style/Management Style,* adapted.

❑ I see myself as more *task-oriented*
❑ I see myself as more *relationship-oriented*

Task-oriented individuals are ruled more by their thinking, with their emotions well under control. Their self-image is developed as a result of the tasks they accomplish. They usually feel their best when they are getting something done, whether at work or at home.

Relationship-oriented individuals are ruled more by their feelings, with more responsive emotions. Their self-image is developed by the acceptance of others. They feel best when they are involved in positive relationships, whether at work or at home.

As with the ask and tell traits, neither the task nor relationship trait is better than the other; each is merely descriptive of two generally different behaviors.

At this point you should have selected either *ask* or *tell* and either *task* or *relationship*. Chart 12-C displays the four basic social styles based on the ask/tell and the task/relationship concept.

Chart 12-C

Ask/Task	Tell/Task
ANALYTICAL	**DRIVER**
Ask/Relationship	Tell/Relationship
AMIABLE	**EXPRESSIVE**

If you selected *ask* and *task,* your social style would be *Analytical.* If you selected *tell* and *task*, your social style would be *Driver.* If you selected *ask* and *relationship*, your social style would be *Amiable.* If you selected *tell* and *relationship*, your social style would be *Expressive.* No specific social style is better than the other (although you are most likely thinking that yours rules!). Each style differs in emphasis and priorities.

Speaking Styles

Each social style will have certain tendencies when speaking or presenting. Examine each style below and see which areas need improvement. Your areas of strength will obviously need less attention than your potential weaknesses.

Analytical Speakers

Analyticals are precise and experts in the area of technique. They like a lot of detail and want to provide all of the facts available. They usually love charts and graphs and often have outstanding visual aids. However, their visual aids can often contain way too much information and overload the audience.

The Analytical speaking style is exacting and intelligent. They have to strive harder to "connect" with the audience, as their presentations are often full of facts and statistics. They also need to work on being more expressive and passionate about their topics. Below are some basic strengths and weaknesses of the Analytical speaker:

Strengths of the Analytical Speaker:
- Starts on time
- Ends on time
- Provides facts and details
- Uses good visual aids
- Answers audience questions thoroughly
- Will not "wing it" in a presentation
- Orderly and organized
- Comes across as thoroughly educated on subject matter

Potential Weaknesses of the Analytical Speaker:
- May appear apathetic
- Can be monotone
- Overloads audience with too many facts
- May talk too slowly
- May depend too heavily on visual aids

- Needs to add spark and charisma to presentations
- Needs to entertain audience a little more
- Needs to work on eye contact
- Needs to be more expressive in body language
- Needs to smile more

Driver Speakers

Drivers are obsessed by a strong compulsion to perform and be in control. They take pleasure in almost any kind of work because it involves activity. Idleness will destroy Drivers. They desire to control and master everything they do. They speak with precision and are not redundant.

Drivers are fast-paced and get to the point. They exude self-confidence on just about any topic. They are great at "winging it," and thinking on their feet. Drivers are great debaters and can often win people over to their point of view through logical debate. Drivers also need to work on "connecting" with the audience, as they are not overly sensitive people. They can often come across as arrogant and cocky if they are not careful. Below are some basic strengths and weaknesses of the Driver speaker:

Strengths of the Driver Speaker:

- Starts on time
- Ends on time
- Gets to the point
- Can be a dynamic presenter
- Outgoing and self-assured
- Remembers materials very well
- Maintains an organized presentation
- Makes excellent eye contact
- Has confident body language
- Appears to be an "authority" on the subject

Potential Weaknesses of the Driver Speaker:

- May appear cocky or arrogant
- Doesn't always reach the audience on an "emotional" level
- May become impatient with incessant questions
- Does not like to be wrong—may argue with audience members
- Doesn't like detail—may miss typos in presentation
- May appear insensitive or abrupt
- May come on too strong for audience
- May cut off audience members during a question and finish their sentence
- Needs to smile more

Amiable Speakers

Amiables are very likeable people who support others. They work well with others and promote harmony. They are found wrapped up in causes. They like to work with words and often influence large groups through writing. Amiables are very compassionate with those who may be hurting. They are patient, good listeners, and are filled with integrity.

The Amiable speaker is calm, cool, and collected. Amiables can be quiet but witty. They tend to be reserved in nature and not very outgoing. They need to stretch themselves in the area of being expressive when presenting. They often speak softly and can appear unenthusiastic. Below are some basic strengths and weaknesses of the Amiable speaker:

Strengths of the Amiable Speaker:

- Relaxed and calm
- Connects with the audience
- Is sympathetic to others
- Avoids controversy
- Tries to make everyone happy
- Appears very sincere about the topic

- Comes across as friendly and approachable
- Is easily liked

Potential Weaknesses of the Amiable Speaker:
- Not very disciplined about time
- May appear apathetic or unenthusiastic
- Avoids controversial topics
- Avoids controversial questions from audience
- May not appear self-confident
- May not project voice enough
- May not persuade audience to action
- Needs to work on eye contact
- Needs to work on more expressive body language

Expressive Speakers

Expressives are very impulsive people who love to socialize. They like to try the new and different. They like to live for the here and now. Expressives have happy and charismatic spirits and can endure hardships and trials easier than the other social styles.

Expressives are friendly, giving, and easygoing. As speakers, they usually make the best storytellers. They are animated and outgoing. They love to use their hands when presenting. They can often exaggerate information and have to focus on sticking to the point. They can go off on tangents and don't particularly care for time constraints. Expressives are the most natural entertainers and speakers. Below are some basic strengths and weaknesses of the Expressive speaker:

Strengths of the Expressive Speaker:
- Outgoing and animated
- Self-assured
- Gets the audience laughing and having fun
- Appears enthusiastic and passionate about topic
- Emotional and demonstrative

- Energetic and charismatic
- Easily "connects" with the audience
- Very persuasive speakers
- Natural on stage
- Good eye contact and body language

Potential Weaknesses of the Expressive Speaker:
- May be unorganized in presentation
- Can over-exaggerate information
- May overwhelm some audiences
- Can talk too loud at times, or even shout
- Can appear overly emotional
- Easily distracted
- May have too much entertainment in presentation and not enough substance
- Doesn't listen carefully to audience questions
- May not provide enough fact and detail

As you can see, each speaker style has areas of strength and weakness. To become a truly great speaker, you have to adopt some of the traits and characteristics of all four styles when speaking. Certain traits or techniques may not come naturally for you, but practice and perseverance will equip you with exactly what you need.

The next chapter will provide you with some specific tools and techniques for appealing to all four social styles when giving presentations. Years of experience have taught me to be all things to all people when giving a presentation. While you will never make everyone 100% happy, you can certainly move much closer to that goal by making a few simple changes.

"It's better to shoot for the moon and hit an eagle, than to shoot for an eagle and hit a rock."

—Unknown

13

THE FOUR TYPES
OF PEOPLE IN
THE AUDIENCE

"Anyone taken as an individual, is tolerably
sensible and reasonable- as a member of a crowd,
he at once becomes a blockhead."
—*Friedrich von Schiller*

Now that you know what type of speaker you are, you need
to examine your audience. Every audience will contain the four
main social styles. I have surveyed hundreds of audiences when
I speak on the social styles concept, and without fail, every audience has all four social styles present. Of course, if you are
speaking to an audience of three, you will prove me wrong on
this issue!

Great presenters are aware of their own tendencies and how to adapt to please a wide range of preferences in the audience. Once you learn the general expectations of each social style, you can modify your presentations to include an element of appeal for each social style. It's not as difficult as you might think.

The Four Kinds of People in the Audience

Every audience will have Analyticals, Drivers, Amiables, and Expressives. Each social style responds differently as a member of the audience. Each social style has different expectations of the speaker, the topic, and the delivery of the information. Below is a description of each style in the audience and how to adapt to meet the specific needs of that style.

Analyticals in the Audience

Analyticals can be very critical of speakers. They expect you to know your stuff and have the facts to back up your statements. They have high standards and are perfectionists. They are looking for content above entertainment.

Analyticals tend to over-analyze presentations, and have a lot of questions. They are not usually bold enough to blurt out questions, so it's important to facilitate question and answer segments throughout your presentation. A simple, "Does anyone have any questions so far?" will go a long way to please the Analyticals.

Analyticals may take the speaker off on a tangent with overly technical questions. If you experience this, the best way to handle it is to briefly answer the question and then offer to discuss it in more detail at the break.

Most Analyticals do not like to draw attention to themselves. They don't like to be selected to demonstrate something or answer a question. They will definitely not be the first ones to volunteer for something in a presentation setting.

Analyticals love detail, graphs, and charts. It's important to incorporate some of these into your presentation. However, you don't want to bore everyone else who could care less about detail, so use it sparingly. The way to make the Analytical happy in this area is to provide additional information in handouts.

If you want to adapt to meet the needs of the Analyticals in your audience, try some of these techniques:

- Don't make blanket statements
- Don't over-generalize
- Have the facts and statistics to back up your topic
- Provide some graphs and charts
- Explain the "why's"
- Make sure your information is accurate
- Don't push Analyticals to participate
- Don't speak too loud or too fast
- Remain patient with their questions
- Stay on schedule
- Have an organized presentation
- Don't get overly emotional
- Don't spend a lot of time on "chit-chat"
- Stay business-like

Drivers in the Audience

Drivers get very antsy during presentations. They have a hard time sitting in one place for an extended period of time. They need to be involved in lots of activity, and they don't do well in "lecture" environments.

The Drivers in the audience will assimilate and assess information very quickly. They expect speakers to move along quickly from point to point and not belabor an issue. They get bored very easily in presentations and are often found reading ahead in the handouts (which is why it's a good idea to give the handouts out after the presentation).

Drivers are often sitting through presentations reluctantly and expect the speaker to have something very valuable to say. They are also looking for content above entertainment as the Analytical does. They are often thinking about all of the things they need to get done, and their top priority is to save time. Drivers get very irritated by speakers who waste their time.

Drivers expect presenters to start and end on time and be organized in their presentation. They want the speaker to have a point and get to it quickly. Drivers often challenge speakers about their topic or knowledge. Don't let this alarm you. Simply compliment them on their question or their level of knowledge and address them with confidence. Drivers don't always expect you to agree with them, but they do expect you to take a stand and stick by your point of view.

Drivers don't mind demonstrating as a volunteer and will do it with confidence. They grasp concepts, instructions, and activities very quickly. They will also be great group leaders if you have team activities in your presentations. Drivers will take the bull by the horns and move people to action.

If you want to adapt to meet the needs of the Drivers in your audience, try some of these techniques:

- Start on time
- Have an organized presentation
- Know your material
- Don't talk slowly or monotone
- Don't belabor your points
- Speak with confidence
- Use strong body language
- Don't appear wishy-washy
- Keep the presentation moving
- Provide some activities
- Let the Drivers lead in team activities
- Answer questions with confidence and authority
- Don't get overly emotional
- Make sure your humor, props, and visual aids all have a point
- Stay business-like

Amiables in the Audience

Amiables are great audience members. They are very affirming and smile a lot. They make speakers feel good about themselves. They are quiet and pay attention to what the speaker is saying.

The Amiables in the audience prefer to observe. They will be the last ones to ever volunteer for an activity or demonstration. They don't like to be put on the spot, and they don't like to be the center of attention. They prefer to learn by watching instead of participating.

Amiables are easily moved by emotional stories. They appreciate speakers who will attempt to connect with the listeners. They are very receptive to emotional speakers and value personal stories and experiences that are shared by the speaker. They also value speakers who show concern and respect for the audience.

When presenting to Amiables, they want to know how your information will affect the relationships in their lives, even if it's work-related. They are more interested in people than tasks, and they relate new learning experiences to the relationships in their lives.

The Amiables will never challenge the speaker or stir up controversy. In fact, if they know other people in the group who are making waves, Amiables will often attempt to keep the peace. If you want to adapt to meet the needs of the Amiables in your audience, try some of these techniques:

- Be sincere
- Share personal stories
- Connect with your audience
- Don't come on too strong or overwhelm
- Ask if anyone has questions
- Don't ask them to volunteer for activities
- Don't push them to participate
- Show them how to apply information to their relationships

- Explain the "why's"
- Provide social encounters for them (frequent breaks)
- Smile frequently
- Don't shout
- Show your personable side
- Use team activities to involve them
- Use colorful graphs and charts

Expressives in the Audience

Expressives are usually the disrupters in the class. They are social butterflies, and they love to talk. It's very difficult for them to sit still and be quiet. They usually think of something funny to say, and they just have to share it with the person next to them.

They are usually the first ones to volunteer for an activity or exercise. They don't mind getting up in front of people, and they certainly don't mind being the center of attention.

Expressives like to share their own experiences in presentations if the setting allows. Speakers are often faced with the challenge of reining in the Expressives and staying on track with the presentation. They are restless and full of energy, so they become bored easily if the speaker is dull or monotone.

Expressives love to tell stories and they can appreciate a speaker who tells stories. They love animation and flamboyancy. Expressives like to be entertained and they love to laugh. They are usually the ones who provide a good amount of natural humor from the audience. They say and do funny things and are usually happy-go-lucky.

Expressives are emotional beings and are stirred by emotional stories. They are usually the first ones to shed a tear in the audience or burst out in laughter. They are not afraid to share their emotions and appreciate speakers who will show their human side. If you want to adapt to meet the needs of the Expressives in your audience, try some of these techniques:

- Tell stories
- Be entertaining
- Use humor
- Allow for social interactions
- Leave time for discussions
- Smile
- Provide interactive activities
- Keep it fast-paced
- Use more expressive body language
- Allow them to volunteer and participate
- Spotlight them when you can
- Use colorful visual aids
- Give them something to do (write on the flip chart, pass out handouts, etc.)
- Limit your statistical information

As you can see, each social style is looking for something a little different from the presenters. If you add a little bit for each social style, you will have a more well-balanced presentation. Yes, it takes a little extra work, but it's worth it!

14

WHAT TO DO WHEN THINGS GO WRONG

"Anything that can go wrong will go wrong."
—*Murphy's Law*

Τhis is a very easy chapter to write, because I have had so many things go wrong throughout the years. Anyone who gives presentations frequently enough will experience unexpected problems. It's a normal part of speaking. All speakers have to experience failed equipment, forgetting their material, room distractions, or rude audience members. This chapter will address some of the more common problems that speakers may encounter.

Equipment Failure

Presenters should always be prepared for equipment failure. I have had projection lamps burn out during my presentation. I have had my laptop freeze up on me in the middle of a Power-Point slide transition. I have arrived at a workshop to discover that my laptop was not compatible with the projector of the company. I have watched VCRs eat my video tapes.

The best way to handle an equipment failure is to not depend on it. You should have a backup plan to make your presentation without the equipment. Another option is to have backup equipment. Most people don't carry around extra laptops or projectors, but it's not a bad idea. If an organization has a projector, I will use it. However, I will also bring my own as a backup when I can. I often carry an extra laptop computer or I will put all of my presentations on a thumb drive when it's not feasible to carry two laptops.

No matter what the equipment failure is, it's always best to handle it with humor. Joking about it relieves the stress and tension of the situation, and lets the audience know that you don't take yourself too seriously. Once you show that you can present without it or you have a backup plan, the audience is very understanding.

If you need time to move to your backup plan or make adjustments to conduct your presentation without the equipment, take a break. It's a great time to let the audience have a short recess while you solve the problem. Again, the key is to stay light-hearted about it and assure the audience that you always have a backup plan.

Room Distractions

Every speaker has to cope with room distractions. Some distractions cannot be avoided, but some can. If you have to speak during a meal, arrange it so you are speaking before or after the meal. It's very difficult to compete with food! People are asking for the salt to be passed, knives are scraping on the plates, and dishes are clanging together as the waiters clear tables. It's very difficult for people to give you their undivided attention if their attention is divided with food.

Other distractions may be unavoidable. Maybe someone has a cell phone ring or a beeper go off. Sometimes people in the back of the room begin talking and don't realize how loud they are. I have had alarms go off, blinds fall off windows, janitors walking through the room, loud crashes, conspicuous belches, chainsaws blaring out the window, and every other distraction you can imagine.

No matter what the distraction is, the first rule is to *acknowledge it!* Until you do, the audience will stay hung up on it and will not be listening to you. By acknowledging the distraction, you can then move on. The best way to acknowledge most distractions is through the use of humor. A joking wise-crack about a distraction puts the audience at ease and keeps the mood light.

Foot-in-Mouth

I have certainly had my fair share of sticking my foot in my mouth. I have said the wrong thing at the wrong time and blatantly embarrassed myself. This is the best time ever to laugh at yourself—everyone else will! Don't take yourself so seriously that you can't acknowledge when you have stuck your foot in your mouth.

The worst foot-in-mouth scenario is when your blunder involves a member of the audience. I had someone ask me a question once and in the midst of my answer I made a wisecrack about IRS auditors. The person turned out to be an IRS auditor. Boy, did I feel stupid! What were the chances of *that*? I humbly apologized and made fun of myself. Luckily, he had a great sense of humor, but my face was red, nonetheless.

The best way to keep your foot out of your mouth is to choose your words carefully. I have learned to not mock *any* occupation, as I may end up with that very occupation in my audience. I have also learned to stay clear of certain topics to avoid sticking my foot in my mouth. If my foot inadvertently ends up in my mouth anyway, it's still best to handle it with a lot of humility and a little humor.

You Forget Your Material

There have been many times I have forgotten sections of my presentation. If I am using PowerPoint, this doesn't happen because I can navigate through my presentation in an organized manner. As each slide comes up, I am reminded what to say next. If I am presenting from memory, this is more of a challenge.

The audience has no idea how your presentation is supposed to flow. The best way to handle forgotten material is to just move on to something else. Don't stand there looking awkward and confused until you remember it. The audience will never know you forgot part of your presentation unless you tell them. I watched a presentation once where the speaker just stopped in the middle of it and said, "Wow, this has never happened to me before. I have completely forgotten my speech and what I was going to say."

This let the audience know that he had a "canned" and memorized speech (well, memorized until he forgot it!). Had he just moved on to another area that he remembered, we would have been none the wiser. Learning to think on your feet and speak impromptu will come in handy when you forget your material. Just move on.

Your Jokes Bomb

It's painful to watch a speaker attempt humor and have it fail. It's even more painful to see a speaker stress out about it. It adds more tension to the room and makes it even more difficult for people to lighten up and laugh.

Sometimes it takes awhile for an audience to warm up and lighten up. It's a real chore to get them laughing in the morning, so don't put a lot of effort into it at that time of the day. Sometimes audiences just don't get the joke, or you messed up the timing and they didn't know they were supposed to laugh.

I have thrown out some humor and been greeted with silence. I have watched the blank stare on the faces of the audience after making a joke. I always handle it with more humor. My favorite way to address it is to say, "Okay, if you're not going to laugh at my jokes, I'll just keep telling them!" That always gets a good chuckle, and eases my tension if the audience didn't get my humor. I may also let the moment of silence exist and then I look down at the palm of my hand. I act as if it is a tablet and I use an invisible pen in the other hand to scribble in my palm as I lower my voice and say, "Note to self... don't use that joke." That always gets a good chuckle too.

There's also another way to address missed or bombed humor: ignore it. Sometimes the audience doesn't know they were supposed to laugh or you were trying to be funny. If you simply move on and don't draw attention to it, the audience may never know you were attempting humor. This only works if you didn't make a blatant attempt at humor and then bombed. In that case, you need to acknowledge it with humor and move on.

It can be a very stressful experience to have humor bomb in public speaking. One way to avoid this is to try out your humor on others first. It's very risky to try out a new joke on a public audience before you have tried it out on others. If no one thinks the joke is funny, don't bother using it in a public speaking venue.

You Make a Fool of Yourself

I was speaking at the front of a large crowd one afternoon. I had a lot of technological equipment hooked up at the front of the room. As I was crossing over from one side of the room to the next, my foot got caught up in some of the electrical cords, and I tripped. I caught myself before I fell to the ground, but I can assure you, I looked like a complete idiot.

The audience always feels bad for the speaker when something like this happens, and may even become stressed about it if the speaker doesn't handle it properly. Deep down, they really want to laugh about it, but they also don't want to offend the speaker. The best thing you can do is lead them in the laughter (unless of course something other than your pride is really hurt). I usually make some wise crack like "I also juggle and do magic," or "My friends call me Grace."

On another occasion, I was very rambunctiously and expressively telling a story about how I wanted to kick my car. As I was making the kicking motion with my leg, my shoe flew off. It went soaring through the air and nearly nailed a police officer in the head. The room burst out in laughter and I didn't miss a beat. I looked at the officer and said, "Will you reconsider that speeding ticket you gave me this morning?"

Humor always lightens the mood in the room, and it keeps people awake. When you inadvertently make a fool of yourself, use it as an opportunity to tie in some humor. Believe me, the first thing that comes to mind when speakers make fools of themselves is laughter, so your best bet is to let them laugh.

Rude Audience Members

Anyone who has had the opportunity to speak before enough audiences has had to cope with rude audience members. Training workshops tend to lend themselves to more interactivity, which in turn can bring out some of the rudeness I am referring to.

I have had people continue to "chit-chat" during a presentation. I'm not talking about an occasional leaning over and whispering something to the person next to you. I'm talking about full-blown conversations where other people in the audience are starting to get annoyed.

In this type of situation, I usually try to make light of it and address it quickly. I might say jokingly, "Is there something you two would like to share with the rest of us?" Or, "Do I need to separate you two?" Again, I do it lightheartedly, and my tone is not offensive. I have never had anyone get offended, and most people get the message and stop.

In a few rare instances, I have had people continue to be disruptive. In those cases, if my humor doesn't solve the problem,

I will move to Plan B. I will take a break and then privately speak with the disrupting audience members. I may also find something for one of them to do so I can separate them (for example, I might ask one of them to come up and write on the flip charts). If none of those techniques work, I kick my shoe off and hope it hits them in the head (kidding).

I spent five years conducting training and instructional classes on financial planning. Without fail, I would always end up with someone in the class who was "challenging." These are the people who ask questions, but they are not really asking a question. What they are really doing is attempting to show the rest of the audience their level of knowledge on the topic or challenge your level of knowledge.

It becomes obvious to everyone in the room what their intentions are. They will often go off on tangents and attempt to dominate discussions. I read a suggestion somewhere for situations like this: "Put them in their place. Call these people on the carpet and embarrass them. Let them know that you are fully aware that they are not asking a genuine question and they are simply trying to make you look bad or make themselves look good."

I'm not sure what kind of speaker would ever suggest doing this, but it's extremely bad advice! Never reprimand or embarrass an audience member. It only makes you look like the jerk, and you would stand a very high chance of hurting your speaking reputation.

I have had to deal with many people in these types of situations and I have never had to be rude to them or "put them in their place." Instead, I publicly validate their level of knowledge and expertise (which is really what they are looking for), and then provide a brief answer to their question. If they continue to press, which is often the case, I may say, "We're delving into a pretty complex aspect of this topic, and in an effort to keep with the agenda and get you out of here on time tonight, how about if you and I discuss that at the break or after the class is over?" I've never had anyone refuse that request, and it allows the challenging audience member to save face.

There is never any reason to be rude as a speaker, even if you have to deal with a rude audience member. I can assure you that if someone in the audience is rude enough, other members of the audience will do something about it. I have seen this happen, and it allows the speaker to save face and maintain a positive reputation.

Apathetic Applause after the Introduction

Nothing sets a bad tone for a presentation more than apathetic applause after an introduction. Even worse than apathetic applause is no applause. I can tell you from experience that apathetic or no applause after an introduction is the direct result of an apathetic introduction.

A strong introduction sets the stage for your presentation. Good speakers will invest some time and energy into developing an introduction that establishes their areas of expertise and prepares the audience for an outstanding presentation. The best way to assure this happens is to write your own introduction and then ask the person who is introducing you to read it word-for-word.

Many speakers just send over a biography to the program coordinator and tell them to take whatever information they need from the biography to do the introduction. This is a bad idea. The introduction will come across dry and uninteresting. If you write the introduction specifically for each speaking engagement, you can inspire the audience to listen with anticipation. The introduction should address what you will be talking about, why you are an expert in this area, and how it will benefit the listeners. This is what inspires applause.

It's not enough to write your own biography. You must also communicate the importance of the introduction to the person who will be introducing you. You need to let them know that it is important to establish your credibility as a speaker and to prepare the audience for the presentation.

The person introducing you needs to understand that he/she will be setting the stage for your presentation. This person needs to understand the importance of a strong and enthusiastic introduction. After reading your introduction with enthusiasm, the person introducing you needs to say something like, "Please join me in a round of applause," or "Please join me in welcoming...."

I will usually write this part into my introduction so the person understands the importance of leading the audience in applause. There is nothing worse than walking to the front of a room or on to a stage in the midst of silence. It's intimidating for the speaker and uncomfortable for the audience.

A good round of applause will also get the blood pumping in the audience members and wake them up a little. This is especially helpful if you are not the first speaker. There's much more energy in the room after a good round of applause, so make sure your introduction facilitates this.

There have been some situations where I have gone through everything I just suggested, and I still get an apathetic introduction because the person introducing me did not read my introduction and did not lead the audience in applause. This poses a special challenge for the speaker, but there are two things you can do. The first thing you need to do is exert a little extra enthusiasm and energy in the beginning of your presentation to compensate.

The second thing you can do is acknowledge the people who put on the event and ask everyone to give them a huge round of applause. This increases the energy level in the room and sets a more positive stage.

Typos or Misspellings in Your Presentation

I was scheduled to speak at a corporation, and two days before my presentation, the program coordinator asked me to make major changes to the presentation. She wanted some specific information added, and wanted me to address some issues that were hot topics in their company at that time.

I was overloaded with work the next two days, so I ended up spending the evening before my presentation updating my PowerPoint slides. That was a bad idea. I cannot proof my own work, and I inevitably miss typos and misspellings. Under normal circumstances, I would have someone else look through my slides or I would go through them with a magnifying glass. I didn't get the chance to do either, and I surely regretted it the next day. My presentation had no less than five typos in it, and I wanted to crawl in a hole and cover myself up with dirt!

Luckily, I had established a light-hearted environment with a lot of humor. I continued to joke about the "alternative" ways to spell words that maybe they weren't aware of yet. It became a source of humor for the rest of the training session. I learned a valuable lesson about making sure my PowerPoint slides were correct. Some mistakes will be inevitable, and humor is the best way to handle it.

Always have someone else proof your presentation visual aids. Have someone look over your handouts for errors and typos. If you still miss something, acknowledge it and use it as a source of humor. Self deprecation is the best form of humor there is!

As you can see, when something goes wrong, humor is usually the best way to handle it. Regardless of the situation, your audience is much more likely to handle something in stride if you do. So the next time something goes wrong, choose humor over stress.

15

ATTENTION TO DETAIL

"Show me a man who cannot bother to do little
things and I'll show you a man who cannot be
trusted to do big things."
—*Lawrence D. Bell*

I walked into the seminar with expectations of a useful day. I was about to spend four hours of my valuable time listening to a speaker talk about time management. I am always looking for ways to become more efficient, and I hate to waste time.

The room was set up with folding chairs in straight rows across the floor. There was one aisle down the middle with a long table at the front of the room. Scattered across the table were papers, pens, a few props, and a can of soda. People were spread all over the room with many empty seats throughout the room. I selected an empty seat towards the back of the room.

The presenter started the seminar with a dry greeting and an explanation of where the bathrooms were located. Someone coughed and it echoed throughout the room. The walls were bare and the ceiling was high. The room felt hollow and empty.

As the seminar progressed, the presenter asked us to write down how we spent our time. I was trying to balance a notepad on my lap as I hunched over my chair. The people around me were doing the same thing. There was no interaction and the room felt lifeless.

After about two hours, I was dying of thirst and needed to use the restroom. I quietly slipped out the back door to find the nearest restroom. I then hunted down some water. By the time I returned to my seat, I had missed about fifteen minutes of the presentation. The speaker finally decided to offer a break. Just my luck!

The four hours seemed to drag on and it took everything I had to stay in my seat and finish the workshop. It started to get muggy and warm in the room, and people were getting fidgety in their seats. The speaker continued to "lecture" to the audience, not noticing a few people nodding off. I guess he didn't notice a few people slipping out and never coming back either.

While there were bits and pieces of valuable information in that four-hour seminar, it was a very painful process to get that information. The seminar could have been improved drastically with a few minor changes and some attention to detail.

Far too many presenters feel that valuable information speaks for itself, and people should be willing to sit in a chair for four hours to glean that information. Unfortunately, it just doesn't work that way. If you want people to walk away from your presentation with a positive experience in their minds, you need to make some extra effort.

The best presentations reflect an attention to detail. Good speakers make sure every detail is attended to, and they take the responsibility themselves. They may delegate certain tasks to others in the process of setting up a seminar or a presentation, but the speaker owns the ultimate responsibility for a great delivery.

When giving presentations, there are certain details that should be considered. Some of the more important areas to examine are listed below. When all of these factors are taken into consideration, your presentation will have that extra life breathed into it!

Room Setup

Room setup is often neglected when giving presentations, and it's very important. The setup of the room will be one of the factors that determine the amount of interactivity that takes place, the energy level of the audience, and the overall ambiance.

If you will be conducting an interactive seminar that requires a lot of writing, tables should be used for the attendees to write on. Tables are traditionally arranged as indicated in chart 15-A.

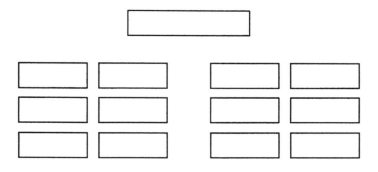

Chart 15-A (the traditional room setup for tables)

I do not recommend this type of setup. Attendees are forced to look at the back of each other's heads, and there is not a lot of room for interaction in the event you offer hands-on activities. People tend to enjoy presentations more when they can see the faces of other people in the room. This creates a warmer atmosphere and raises the energy level. I've tested this out on hundreds of audiences, and, believe me, it's true!

A more appropriate setup for tables would be either a "chevron style" as shown in chart 15-B, or a "horseshoe style" as shown in chart 15-C. When you arrange tables in a manner that allows attendees to see each other, the result is a more lively room of people.

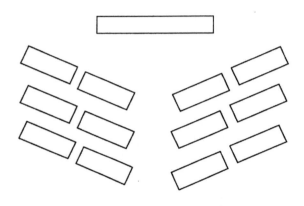

Chart 15-B (the chevron room setup)

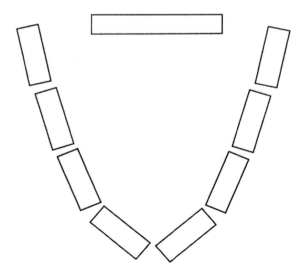

Chart 15-C (the horseshoe room setup)

If you are not using tables in your presentation, you still need to consider how the chairs will be arranged. A traditional room setup with only chairs is depicted in chart 15-D. Chairs are placed next to each other in straight rows across the room with an aisle down the middle.

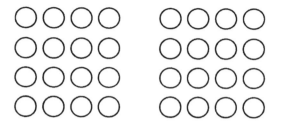

Chart 15-D (traditional room setup with only chairs)

This type of arrangement does not allow the audience members to see the faces of other members in the audience. Instead, it creates a feeling of isolation. A better setup for the chairs would be a semi-circle arrangement that allows audience members to see each other. This increases the energy level in the room and adds some liveliness. Chart 15-E depicts a semi-circle setup.

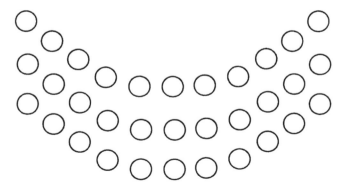

Chart 15-E (Semi-circle room setup with only chairs)

When setting up chairs, it is always better to put out less chairs than you think you will need versus setting up too many. When you have far more chairs than you will need, the audience tends to spread out all over the room, and it creates a sense of emptiness. When you fill up the chairs in the room, you will keep people closer together.

If you have to add more chairs, this will only add to the excitement of the presentation. It gives a sense of crowdedness and popularity for the presentation. It's much better than having to ask everyone to move to the front of the room because so many chairs are empty.

In addition to the tables and chairs, you need to pay attention to the room decor. A dry, drab, and hollow room makes for a dull environment. Look for ways to liven up the room. If you are not good at this, ask someone who is. Some practical ways to liven up a room or bring some warmth to it:

- Tie helium balloons to the edges of the stage or the speaker's table (just make sure they do not block anyone's view)

- Put a balloon arch at the entrance of the room and/or the front of the room

- Bring in some silk plants and scatter them throughout the edges of the room and across the front of the room

- Hang some interesting artwork on the walls

- Cover bare walls with colorful material

- Use nice table cloths on the tables

- Put confetti on tables

- Put centerpieces on tables

Speakers often have a table at the front of the room where they keep their props or reference materials. I usually use a six foot table, and I also put my water and throat lozenges on this table. If you want to keep the room looking nice and professional, put a podium/table wrap on top of this table to hide props and materials. I actually had someone custom design one of these for me.

It was made out of white pre-cut shelving that was cut again to meet my specifications. My company name and logo was then painted on it in full color. The table wrap is 3' long and 9" high. It has hinges on each end of it so the outside pieces of the wrap fold in for easy storage. Chart 15-F depicts an image of what the table wrap looks like.

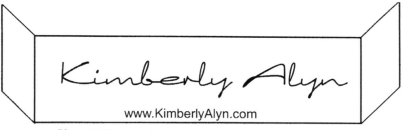

Chart 15-F (sample podium/table wrap for top of table)

These types of table wraps add a higher level of professionalism. Additionally, if you use magic tricks in your presentation as I sometimes do in workshops, it allows you to hide all of your gimmicks behind the wrap. You don't have to bend down and pull something out of a box, or go behind a curtain to get your props ready. It's simple and professional, and it's actually very easy to make.

Once you have all of the tables and chairs set up and the room ambiance taken care of, you need to consider the comfort of your audience. There are a few simple things you can do to ensure the audience is content and comfortable during your presentation.

Audience Comfort

When attendees first enter the room, they are often unsure or uncomfortable with the new surroundings. As a "detail-oriented" presenter, you can help alleviate some of this by adding some distractions for the attendees.

As I mentioned earlier, I have a video slide show running on a huge screen as people come in and sit down. It's a PowerPoint presentation set to "auto mode." It loops through a presentation of about sixty slides until I stop it. Each slide has a funny video file with sound that projects through the sound system. Each video clip is less than fifteen seconds long, and all of the clips are very humorous.

This provides something for the audience to do while they are waiting for the program to start. It also gets them in a great mood, as most of the audience members have had a good laugh before I even get started. It livens up the room and sets the tone for the rest of the presentation.

Another way to put the audience at ease is to greet them at the door. As the speaker, I try to introduce myself to as many people as possible and welcome them to the presentation. If I am at a conference and I know people have a choice of classes to attend, I always thank them for choosing to take my class. I also make myself available at the breaks and after the presentation to talk to audience members. This also adds to their level of comfort and helps to ensure a positive experience. No one likes sitting through a presentation with a self-absorbed, stuck-up presenter.

There are a few other things you can do to ensure the comfort of your audience:

- **Provide water or other beverages:** When conducting seminars, I always provide water, coffee, and tea. I offer caffeinated and de-caffeinated coffee and tea. Depending on the time of day, I may also offer different types of soda. I don't recommend providing straws with beverages though. Some people might decide to start catapulting spit wads across the room. It's a huge temptation when that straw is sitting right there on the table, so do everyone a favor and remove the temptation—no straws!

- **Provide frequent breaks:** I try to offer a break every hour. Because I offer lots of beverages, bathroom breaks are a necessity! Besides, it gets people up and moving and keeps them from getting bored. There's nothing worse than sitting through a long presentation with no breaks *(well I guess there are worse things, but it's still pretty bad!)*. The less interactive a presentation is, the more breaks your audience will need. If your presentation has lots of activities and attendees are moving around or changing positions often, you won't need as many breaks. I would never suggest going past ninety minutes without a break, no matter how interactive the presentation is.

- **Offer snacks:** If I have seminars or workshops that last more than two hours, I will usually have a table with some cookies and fruit (nothing too heavy, because I don't want the attendees getting lethargic from eating too much food).

- **Monitor the temperature:** Room temperature plays a very big role when it comes to the comfort of your audience. A room that is too cold or too hot will annoy your listeners. Make sure someone is keeping an eye on the controls and keeping the room at a comfortable temperature.

- **Provide writing utensils:** Always have extra pens, pencils, and tablets available. Not everyone remembers to bring theirs, and even if you provide handouts, people usually jot down notes. They may just be writing a grocery list for later, but they need something to write it on!

- **Let them socialize:** When members of the audience know each other a little better, it creates a more comfortable room. If you are conducting a seminar, you can add an activity in the beginning where people introduce themselves. I always have people introduce each other in teams of two. One person asks the other one his/her name, title, and a little known fact about that person. Then they take turns standing up and introducing each other. It breaks the ice in the room and adds a lot of humor in the beginning (especially when someone admits to wearing his sister's clothes in grade school!). If the audience is very large, this type of activity is not practical.

- **Let them ask questions:** Not everyone is comfortable asking questions, but they are less comfortable if the speaker doesn't facilitate questions. Stop every once in awhile and see if anyone has questions. If you're presenting a motivational or inspirational speech, I wouldn't recommend this. If, however, you are conducting a seminar or workshop, this is imperative. Build time into your presentations for question and answer sessions.

- **Give them gifts:** Everyone loves to get a gift or a prize. When conducting seminars, I always have team competitions throughout the workshops. The team with the most points at the end of the seminar wins a prize. I will sometimes give a second or third place prize too. For larger presentations that are not workshops, door prizes work great. Attendees can drop their business cards in a hat or bowl and the speaker can draw it out somewhere in the presentation. I give out free books or other fun gifts. I also give out prizes when audience members answer tough questions correctly.

- **Start on time:** When you start late to accommodate people coming in late, you do two things: 1) you insult and punish the people who showed up on time and 2) you reinforce the behavior of people who always show up late. Start when you say you will start. I usually tell a fun story or interject a little humor into the beginning so latecomers do not miss any of the very pertinent information.

- **End on time:** I know you've seen this point made earlier in this book and it's worth making again. *Never* go over your allotted time. You can give the best presentation in the world, but if you keep an audience past the time they expected, you will annoy them and lose some of your credibility. There has never been a known audience that has become upset with a speaker for ending on time or a few minutes early. If you go over, people may even get frustrated and leave while you are talking. Be kind to your audience and stay within your allotted time.

Paying attention to the details makes all the difference if you want to give a butt kicking presentation. It's the little things that matter, and too many speakers ignore this basic principle. Take the extra time to manage the details of your presentations, and you will notice a huge difference in the audience response. Additionally, your level of professionalism will rise and you will build a reputation as a polished and top-notch presenter!

16

SHARPEN YOUR SKILLS

"The wise learn from the experience of others, and the creative know how to make a crumb of experience go a long way."
—Eric Hoffer

E ven the best speakers in the world need to continue to improve and work on their presentation skills. Whether you are a beginning presenter or a polished professional, there are a variety of ways to continue the improvement process. I want to share some of the best ways I have found to sharpen your public speaking and presenting skills.

- **Join an amateur speaking group:** If you are in the early stages of getting over the fear of public speaking, local speaking groups are an ideal way to accomplish this. These types of organizations provide a supporting and non-threatening atmosphere to get you started.

Toastmasters International is the largest organization for this type of objective, and they have local clubs in different cities and towns throughout the world (toastmasters.org). These clubs will provide you with a weekly or bi-monthly platform to practice your presentation skills. You will meet with other members of the community who are also trying to improve their speaking and presentation skills. This type of speaking group is ideal for those who simply want to overcome the fear of public speaking or who want to improve their basic presentation skills. For more advanced speakers and presenters or professional speakers, I would recommend a professional speaking organization.

- **Join a professional speaking organization:** If you want to really stretch yourself as a presenter, or you want to be a professional speaker, join a professional speaker's association. In these types of organizations, you will be challenged by some of the best speakers in the industry. You will glean knowledge and experience from people who are getting paid to give presentations. Some of these organizations actually require that you speak professionally to join. A great organization to join for professional speakers is the National Speakers Association (nsaspeaker.org). This organization has state and regional chapters throughout the country. They offer a wide variety of educational and certification programs for professional speakers.

- **Get professional coaching:** Executive coaching is available from a variety of sources. Professional speaking coaches can provide you with one-on-one training. When you use a speaking coach, you can progress quickly from an average presenter to an outstanding presenter. A speaking coach will be able to identify your specific weaknesses and work with you to eliminate them. This person will also be able to fine-tune your technique in an effort to eliminate any annoying mannerisms or gestures. A coach will also teach you to take advantage of your own personal style so you can "wow" your audiences with your strengths. Just make sure the coach is someone who actually speaks professionally or has actual experience with public speaking. Avoid "book knowledge coaches" who don't get out and do the actual speaking and presenting.

- **Order tapes and videos:** There is a plethora of tapes and videos available on the subject of public speaking and presenting. The Internet is a great place to find resource information. Just conduct a search under "How to become a better public speaker," and you will have hours of material to wade through! There are plenty of tapes, videos, articles, books, and any other resource materials you can think of.

- **Audio or video tape yourself:** The next time you give a presentation, audio tape it or even video tape it. You will be amazed at how many things you can find to improve just by watching yourself! You'll begin to notice the little mannerisms you have. You might be saying "ah" or "um" too much. You might have a bad habit of clearing your throat every ten seconds. Maybe you touch your nose a lot out of nervousness. You might fidget with a pen or jingle the change in your pocket. Maybe you play with your hair while you are speaking. These are all subconscious things you will be unaware of until you listen to yourself or watch yourself. It's actually a very painful process. I prefer to have others watch the video or listen to the tape for me and then give me suggestions.

- **Use evaluation forms:** If you are conducting seminars or presenting to smaller groups or audiences, use an evaluation form. This will provide you with a lot of feedback about your presentation and the areas that need improvement. If you are a professional speaker, you can also ask for comments about the presentation that can be used in future promotional materials (with the permission of the person who filled out the evaluation form). When I conduct seminars or workshops, I sometimes give out evaluation forms for feedback. I use this information to structure my presentations to meet the needs of the audience. I also receive feedback on my presentation skills and I make changes accordingly. Chart 16-A depicts an example of the front page of my evaluation form. Chart 16-B depicts an example of the backside of the form.

Chart 16-A (the front side of sample evaluation form)

PRESENTER	Not even close	Fair	Very Good	Off the charts!
Communicates concepts well				
Engaging speaker				
Makes topic interesting				
Is knowledgeable in subject matter				
TRAINING CONTENT				
Useful				
Interesting				
Adequate amount of information				
POWERPOINT/REMOTE CONTROL SYSTEM				
Complimented training				
Easy to read and understand				
Used properly by presenter				
OVERALL PRESENTATION				
Met my expectations				
Was worth the time				
Was a professional presentation				

What did you like the most about the presentation?

What did you like the least about the presentation?

Would you like to receive email announcements on any new product releases? If so, please provide your email address here (please note, you will receive no more than one email a month and we do not share your information with anyone):

Chart 16-B (the back side of sample evaluation form)

Can we use any comments below in promotional materials? _____ yes _____ no

If YES, please print your first and last name clearly:

_____

Authorized signature:

_____

Your title:

_____

City and State:

_____

If you were to refer this presentation or the speaker to another organization, what would you say?

_____

_____

_____

_____

Any additional comments you would like to make?

_____

_____

_____

_____

- **Find a mentor:** There are lots of great presenters out there who would love to mentor someone else. Most great presenters had good mentors, and they know the value of mentoring. A good mentor will watch you give presentations and give you some constructive feedback. You don't want some sappy person who is just going to stroke your ego; you want someone to be honest with you and help you improve. You want someone who is bold enough to tell you where your weaknesses exist and how to get rid of them. A good mentor will do this in a positive and constructive way, but they won't waste your time making you feel good about presentations that really stink! I know that's harsh, but that's how you improve. When a real mentor is open and honest with you, you will actually make positive strides in your public speaking skills. Find a good mentor who wants to see you improve.

- **Listen to professional speakers:** If you want to learn new techniques and watch a professional in action, go listen to a professional speaker. Take some time out of your schedule to watch someone else give a great presentation. Find out why the audience loves their style. Observe their technique and the flow of their presentation. Examine their visual aids and the professionalism of the presentation. In which areas are you lacking? In which areas do you already excel? Listen to other speakers with the intent of improving, not becoming like them. Every speaker will have their own flair and style, and you will never be able to perfectly mimic another speaker. Besides, you wouldn't want to anyway. The very thing that will set you apart from other presenters is your individual style and flair.

- **Go to comedy clubs:** If you want to learn how to have better timing in your humor, go visit comedy clubs. There are clubs all over the United States, and some of them still have good, clean humor. This is a great way to see how stories and jokes are pulled off in front of a group of people. You'll also see why some humor bombs and why certain jokes shouldn't be used. I have visited a lot of comedy clubs, and I have learned a great deal in the area of what *not* to do, in addition to ways to improve the use of humor in my presentations.

- **Take PowerPoint classes:** If you use PowerPoint a lot, I highly recommend taking a PowerPoint class. These types of classes are offered all over the country, and they can provide you with some useful tools. You'll learn shortcuts for designing presentations, and some of the capabilities of PowerPoint that you may not have been aware of. You will also learn how to put together a presentation that is appealing to an audience instead of annoying. The more comfortable and familiar you are with your advanced visual aids, the more impressed your audience will be. Audiences become very annoyed by people who attempt to use Power-Point but use it incorrectly.

- **Get out and present more:** The best way to sharpen your skills is to give more presentations! Any fear you may have will slowly dissipate. Any annoying habits and gestures will subside as you become more aware of them. Repetitive words will start to disappear as you become more and more comfortable presenting in front of people. Your skills will sharpen and your presentation will become very polished with practice, patience, and perseverance!

Whether you are setting out to give better presentations in small meetings or you are embarking on a professional speaking career, it's all about style and technique! Each and every one of us has a very unique style of speaking and presenting. As you concentrate on fine-tuning your style, your presentations will improve.

We all have something to offer in the way of a great presentation. Maybe you have some personal stories to help drive your point home. Perhaps there have been some experiences in your life that can inspire or motivate others. Maybe you have a natural charisma that will persuade others to action. Take an inventory of your existing assets, and learn how to incorporate those assets into your presentation. If you are naturally funny and like to tell jokes, incorporate that natural humor into your presentations. If you like magic or juggling, use some of that.

You will discover that certain skills and techniques come more naturally for you while others may need more attention. We all have our specific strengths that need to be capitalized. Additionally, we all have our weaknesses that need to be addressed and improved. As you begin to apply many of the tools and techniques in this book, you will be well on your way to giving butt kicking presentations. Just remember: in all that you do, do it with excellence!

NOW GET OUT THERE AND START GIVING SOME BUTT KICKING PRESENTATIONS!

OTHER SPEAKING RESOURCES BY DR. ALYN

"How to Give a Butt Kicking Presentation" Audio CD

"Dr. Alyn's Hilarious Video Collection"

"How to Deal with Annoying People" Book

To order these products log on to:

Shop.KimberlyAlyn.com

HOW TO ORDER OTHER BOOKS BY DR. ALYN

Log on to any of these sites:
Shop.KimberlyAlyn.com

OR CALL:
800-821-8116

For more information about Dr. Kimberly Alyn and her speaking services, log on to:

KimberlyAlyn.com

HOW TO SCHEDULE DR. KIMBERLY ALYN FOR A SPEAKING ENGAGEMENT

Call:
1-800-821-8116
email:
Info@KimberlyAlyn.com

or *log on to:*
KimberlyAlyn.com

I love the grasshopper.
Grasshoppers can leap 20 times the length of their own
bodies as they soar through the air. I want to learn to soar like
that—far beyond the length of my perceived limitation.